D1489285

CREATIVE WORSHIP IDEAS

Edited by Lois Keffer

Group®

Loveland, Colorado

Western District Resource Library
2517 North Main
North Newton, KS 67117

Creative Worship Ideas

Copyright © 1993 Group Publishing, Inc.
First Printing
All rights reserved. No part of this book may be reproduced in any manner whatsoever without written permission from the publisher, except where noted in the text and in the case of brief quotations embodied in critical articles and reviews. For information write Permissions, Group Books, Box 481, Loveland, CO 80539.

Credits
Edited by Lois Keffer
Cover designed by Bob Fuller and Liz Howe
Interior designed by Dori Walker

Contributors
J. Brent Bill, Michael Capps, Dave Carver, Karen Ceckowski, Drew Crislip, Karen Dockrey, Dick Hardel, Linda Joyce Heaner, Bob Keffer, Lois Keffer, Rick Lawrence, Paul Lessard, Walter H. Mees, Jr., Mike Nappa, Arlo Reichter, Joani Schultz, Thom Schultz

Unless otherwise noted, scriptures are quoted from the Holy Bible, New International Version. Copyright © 1973, 1978, 1984 International Bible Society. Used by permission of Zondervan Bible Publishers.

Library of Congress Cataloging-in-Publication Data
Creative worship ideas / edited by Lois Keffer ; [contributors, J. Brent Bill... et. al.].
   p. cm.
   ISBN 1-55945-099-1
   1. Worship (Religious education) 2. Worship programs. 3. Drama in public worship. I. Keffer, Lois. II. Bill, J. Brent, 1951-
BV29.C74   1992
264'.0083—dc20   92-35024
                            CIP

Printed in the United States of America

CONTENTS

PART THREE: COMPLETE SERVICES

INTRODUCTION

What does worship mean to you? Singing a psalm in a leafy forest-cathedral? Listening in stained-glass splendor as the 16-foot bass of a pipe organ rocks your soul? Standing in awe at the unleashed power and fury of a thunderstorm? Bowing in solitary silence before the Creator of the universe who took time to answer your need?

Worship isn't always predictable. A sudden awareness and appreciation of God's majesty, love and awesome power may take you by surprise as you contemplate motes of dust dancing in a sunbeam. It may stop you in your tracks to admire the glorious, fleeting colors of sunset. It may catch at your voice as the truth of a hymn reverberates in perfect harmony with your soul.

Worship is not passive. It requires a purposeful bending of the will away from all that clamors for attention, to focus on the glory, holiness and grace of God. When something out of the ordinary happens in the course of worship routine, sleepy pew-sitters suddenly snap to attention. Hearts and minds engage to at least evaluate, if not participate in, the unique thing that suddenly brings them face to face with God's truth.

This book is a tool to help worshipers of all ages encounter that wonderful moment of "Aha!" when the glory of God crashes through patterned predictability. Youth leaders all over the country have contributed their very best creative worship ideas—ideas they've used successfully in their youth groups and congregations.

Part One offers nuggets of creative worship that you can incorporate into a typical Sunday morning format or a youth meeting. You'll find fresh, meaningful ideas for the call to worship, music, prayer, scripture reading, teaching and encouraging.

Part Two consists of 10 easy-to-prepare, thought-provoking dramas that can be used in a variety of worship settings.

In Part Three you'll find eight complete worship services on themes such as service, commitment, Christmas and Easter.

Whether your church is traditional or contemporary, you'll enjoy watching the kids in your youth group grow spiritually as they use these resources to lead your congregation in creative, meaningful worship.

Part One

CREATIVE WORSHIP INGREDIENTS

Use these ideas to add a creative spark to Sunday services or youth meetings. Or plan your own creative worship experience using the "Creative Worship Worksheet" on page 42 to combine several ideas from this section.

CREATIVE PRAYERS

Talking to the Creator of the universe is an incredible privilege and is not to be taken lightly. Prayer can take many forms. God is not limited by our habits or lack of imagination! As you plan and draw from these ideas for creative prayers, keep in mind these essentials: a sense of reverence, opportunities to speak to God and opportunities to listen.

ADVENTURE PRAYERS

Take kids on an adventure prayer-walk they'll never forget. Walk to a river or a water faucet, gather kids in a group and ask for God's cleansing. At a stop sign or traffic signal, pray that God will stop kids from doing things that hurt themselves and others. At a crossroads, pray that God will help kids make wise decisions. Gather around an electric pole or meter and pray for God's power. Stand under a large, spreading tree and pray that God will help kids grow and reach out to others.

Finish the adventure prayer by having kids form a circle and hold hands. Say: **Imagine you're holding the hand of someone who's sick ... Now imagine you're praying with someone who's homeless ... Now that person you're praying with is the president of the United States ... Now it's Saddam Hussein. Let's close our adventure prayer by imagining that we're all holding the hand of Jesus.**

Debrief this prayer time by asking:

- **What did you learn about yourself during our adventure prayer?**
- **What made you uncomfortable?**
- **What did you learn about prayer?**
- **How can you use these ideas to make your personal prayer time more meaningful?**

HEADLINE PRAYERS

Record the evening newscast on videotape. Play the tape during your worship time, stopping after each news segment to pray for the people and situations involved. This type of prayer can be very effective in a Sunday morning worship service, with the videotape projected and the people in pews forming prayer clusters.

Use newspapers for a similar prayer time with trios in your youth group. Give each trio a section of newspaper. Have kids scan the newspaper together and pray for the people they read about. Consider having each group write a postcard telling an individual from the news that your church's youth group prayed for him or her.

PERSONALIZED PRAYERS

Familiar prayers from the Bible take on new meaning when they're personalized. Pray the Lord's Prayer in the first person, saying, "Give me this day my daily bread ..." Or pray the Lord's Prayer in pairs, with kids each inserting their partner's name: "Give Allison this day her daily bread ..." Try a similar approach with Psalm 23: "The Lord is Brock's shepherd ..."

SILENT PRAYER-WALKS

Have kids form pairs for a silent prayer-walk. Give each pair a route to walk. Say: **As you walk, pray silently for the people you meet, the people in the houses and buildings you pass and the people in the cars that pass you. Don't give any outward sign that you're praying.**

Have kids return in 20 minutes to discuss their experiences. This kind of prayer can pull kids out of their hyper modes and sensitize them to the needs of others. You may also want to have kids circle the church in a silent prayer-walk before the morning worship service or walk through the halls and pray for people in other classes.

PAIR PRAYERS

Have participants walk around the room as you play music with an emphasis on prayer, such as "Pray for Me" from *i 2 (Eye)* by Michael W. Smith. Ask kids to focus on the words of the song as they walk and listen. When a worshipful mood has been established, stop the music. Have kids each take the hands of the nearest person, bow their head and pray this simple prayer for their partner:

Lord, help (partner's name) **know how special** (he or she) **is.**

Help (partner's name) **to trust every problem to you. Help** (partner's name) **hang in there, even when it's tempting to give up.**

Repeat the process two or three times, encouraging participants to find a new partner each time.

FRUSTRATION BALLOON PRAYERS

Distribute 1×3-inch slips of paper, pencils and balloons. Ask participants to write on their paper slips one frustration or problem they're currently facing. Explain that one other person will see what's been written but that no one will know who wrote what.

Have worshipers tuck their frustration slips inside their balloons, blow up the balloons and tie them. Then gather everyone in a circle and gently toss the balloons. Play soft music as kids work to keep everyone's balloon in the air. When the music stops, discuss how keeping the balloons in the air is like the way we support each other in prayer.

Have everyone pick up a balloon that's a different color than the balloon he or she inflated. Have worshipers pop their balloons and *silently* read the slips inside. Place a cross at the front of the room. Point out how Jesus carried the weight of the world (even our problems) to the cross when he was crucified. Invite participants one by one to take to the cross the frustration slips they're holding and to imagine laying those problems at Jesus' feet.

As this is happening, encourage worshipers to pray silently for the people whose frustration slips they read as well as for the problems they wrote on their own frustration slips.

POPCORN PRAYERS

Have participants stand in a circle. Encourage each person to pray a one-word prayer. It could be "thanks," "help," "joy" or a person's name—God knows what's meant by the word. Kids may pray more than once but no more than one word at a time. The one-word format reduces anxiety about praying aloud and helps participants focus on the thoughts and feelings they want to communicate to God. When appropriate, close with one word: "amen!"

DIRECTED PRAYERS

This prayer calls for participants to bow their heads while the worship leader gives directions indicating how to pray. Directions include:

● Begin with prayers of praise.
● Pray for God's forgiveness.
● Pray for the needs of others.
● Pray for your own needs.

Pause after each direction and allow participants to pray silently or aloud. The dramatic effect of this prayer is achieved when the short directions are followed by silent prayers from the entire group. Close by praying: **Thank you, Father, for hearing our prayers. Amen.**

COMMISSIONING PRAYERS

This prayer offers strength and encouragement for those who are taking on a special responsibility, such as teaching a class or going on a missions trip. Have the person stand, sit or kneel in the center of a circle. Invite other participants to touch the person on the head or shoulders. If your group is very large, form an outer circle so each participant can touch someone who is touching the person in the middle.

Encourage everyone to pray simple prayers of one word or phrase for the person in the middle. Each prayer focuses on something that will empower that person to perform his or her task, such as "strength," "courage" or "peace of mind."

If you're sending a team of kids, pray for them one by one. End your prayer time with a big group hug.

POTTERS PRAYERS

Give each participant a hunk of modeling clay. Invite kids to form the clay into a shape that symbolizes a big concern in their lives. After a few moments, invite those who would like to talk about their clay figures to do so, but don't pressure anyone to share.

Have kids hold their clay figures in their palms as you pray: **Dear Lord, You are the potter and we are the clay. We trust you to take the rough places in our lives and create from them something beautiful. In Jesus' name, amen.**

Encourage kids to keep their clay figures as prayer reminders and to bring them back to the group when they feel God has answered their prayers.

OPEN-EYED PRAYERS

As kids gather for prayer, they love to share prayer requests in detail. Instead of repeating all the requests in a formal prayer time with closed eyes, encourage kids to use the time they spend sharing their requests as open-eyed prayer. Begin by inviting God to hear the requests and praises as kids talk about them. Close with: **Amen, and thank you, Lord, for hearing, understanding and responding.**

POSITIVE PRAYERS

S o often prayer is limited to requests about fixing what's broken. Sometimes it's healthy to limit our prayers to a positive focus using questions like:

● What's gone well lately?

● What routine things that you take for granted would you miss if you didn't have them—things like a loyal friend, a teacher who understands you and a mom or dad who really cares?

● What problem has God helped you fix and what good has come out of it?

 ● In the midst of all your problems, what good still persists?

Close your positive prayer time with a simple chorus of praise, such as "God Is So Good."

PRAYER TOKENS

H ave kids form pairs or trios for prayer. Ask partners or trio members to give each other tokens of friendship that will remind them to pray for each other during the week. Tokens might be a penny, a photo or card from their wallets, or something they make from art supplies you provide. Have pairs and trios re-form the following week to report on the things they prayed about and to give back the tokens they exchanged.

Use this idea with a large group by giving each person a nickel. Ask:

● **How many cents is a nickel worth?**

Say: **A nickel can be worth a lot when it's used the way we're going to use it. Use your nickel as a prayer token to help you remember to pray about five prayer requests from your group for five out of the next seven days.**

Then ask:

● **How can praying for each other bring riches no amount of money can buy?**

Be sure to follow up on the "nickel prayers" in future meetings.

SCRIPTURE READING AND STUDY

We tend to think of God's Word as a carefully bound book with rows of small type set in even columns, when in fact it's incredibly dynamic and powerfully relevant to all areas of our lives. These ideas will help you and your youth group present scripture in exciting new contexts that will capture the imagination of worshipers.

HAPPY FACES

U se Today's English Version of Matthew 5:1-12 for an interesting scripture reading. Assign one teenager to be the reader. The reader will read the passage but never say the word "happy." Whenever the word "happy" appears, another teenager will stand up, face the congregation and make a happy face by using his or her index fingers to pull his or her lips into a smile. That person will hold this position for the entire reading. Each time the word "happy" appears, another teenager stands up and forms a happy face.

SPECIAL DELIVERY

Prepare to read scripture the way you normally would on a Sunday morning. Just before the reader begins, have a teenager dressed as a delivery person burst into the sanctuary with a large, official-looking envelope and shout, "Special delivery!" As the delivery person carries the envelope to the front of the church, the reader asks, "From who?" The delivery person answers, "From God" as he or she hands over the envelope. The reader removes the contents of the envelope (which is the scripture for the day) and reads it to the congregation.

CIRCULAR SKIT

Many of Jesus' parables can be presented in a circular skit with actors miming the action of the parable being read. The reader stands at one side of the sanctuary with a group of actors lined up beside him or her. Each time there is action in the parable, one, two or three actors walk to the center of the platform and mime what's being read. Then they step off the platform, walk around the congregation and take their places in line again as the next actor or actors mime the next action.

Try this idea with the parable of the sower from Matthew 13:1-9, 18-23. "Seeds" can fall on the ground, sprout and then run off the stage. The next group of seeds can be wilted by someone who plays the sun with waving arms representing ominous, scorching rays. When those actors run off, the third group of seeds can sprout, only to be literally choked and carried off the platform by actors playing thorns. The seeds that grow in the good soil can grow a bit taller as the reader reads "thirty, sixty or a hundred times" (the numbers are reversed from scripture). For "he who has ears, let him hear," have everyone run up onto the platform and cup their hands behind their ears.

Repeat the whole sequence adding a teacher who stays on the platform as the reader reads Jesus' explanation of the parable in verses 18-23.

ON LOCATION

Scripture takes on new significance when it's read "on location." Take your group to a river or stream to read and discuss Psalm 1. Visit a pasture of sheep to read Psalm 23. Go to a favorite fishing hole to read in Matthew 4:18-22 about becoming fishers of men. Take a candle to a dark, windowless room to read in John 1 about Jesus being the light of the world. Let kids squish their fingers in a mud puddle as you read in John 9 about Jesus healing a blind man. Go to a landfill to read in Genesis 1 and 2 about God's charge to Adam to care for the earth. Climb a rocky ledge to read Psalm 18, where God is called "my rock, my fortress and my deliverer."

IN YOUR FACE

If your church has a photocopier, have kids take turns planting their faces on it. Make sure kids keep their eyes closed as their faces are being photocopied. Then, with the murky images in hand, read 1 Corinthians 13:12 about seeing a poor reflection now but seeing face to face someday. Or read 2 Corinthians 3:17-18 about reflecting more and more of God's glory with unveiled faces. Pass around a hand mirror and let students compare their photocopied images to the clear images they see in the mirror. Discuss how faith pulls away the veil that prevents us from seeing and understanding God's glory.

WELL-CONNECTED

Pass around a bunch of grapes as you read John 15:1-8. Have each student read a verse, then eat a grape and pass on the Bible and the bunch of grapes to the next person. After the passage has been read, continue passing the grapes around the group. Talk about the importance of being connected to Jesus—the vine—and to each other— the branches.

STARRY, STARRY NIGHTS

Read God's promises to Abraham and Abraham's response in Genesis 15:1-6 as the kids in your group lie flat on their backs looking up at the starry sky. The effect is heightened if you all lie in a grassy field or yard without many street lights nearby. Talk about trusting the God who created the stars and set them in space.

You can create a similar effect with flashlights in a darkened sanctuary. Play soft worship music. Have worshipers aim their flashlights at the ceiling and click them on and off as you read the Genesis 15 passage or Psalm 19.

FOUR FRIENDS

As you read from Mark 2:1-12 the account of Jesus healing the paralytic who was lowered through the roof by friends, have four members of your youth group come down the aisle of the church carrying a fifth person by four corners of a blanket. At the end of the reading, have the person who was carried get up, fold the blanket and walk out of the sanctuary smiling and rejoicing with the four friends.

HOLD THAT KNIFE!

Recruit a father and son (10 years old or younger) to help you dramatize Abraham's test in Genesis 22:1-19. At the appropriate point in the reading, the father walks to the front of the church with his son, then picks up the boy and lays him on the altar. As the reader reads verse 10, the father raises a large knife. Then the reader walks over to the father, grasps his arm and lowers it. The father and son hug each other during the rest of the Bible passage and then return to their seats hand in hand.

Try a similar dramatization of the banishment of Hagar and Ishmael in Genesis 21:8-20. Use a hidden canteen to represent the well that Hagar discovers.

RAP IT

You probably have would-be rap singers in your group. Challenge them to develop a rap using Psalm 100. Since it is poetry, it should work quite well. Once they've given it a try with Psalm 100, encourage them to rap other scriptures. This approach is sure to grab the worshipers' attention!

CLAP IT

Select a scripture that has a frequently used word. First Corinthians 13 is a good example with its emphasis on the word "love." Or use Joshua 1 and the words "strong" and "courageous." Each worshiper will need a copy of the scripture in the same translation. The challenge is to not speak the word but to clap one time wherever the word appears.

This approach is effective with one person reading the scripture and everyone clapping or with everyone reading and clapping. The group will be quite aware of the key word by the time it has clapped its way through the scripture!

SILENCE IT

Have worshipers open their Bibles to a passage with a key word that appears over and over, such as 1 Corinthians 12:12-20 with the word "body," John 15:1-8 with the word "fruit," or John 15:9-17 with the word "command." Have the group read the passage aloud but pause in silence whenever the key word appears. You may have the group read the passage several times, a bit faster each time. This discipline helps everyone focus on the key word.

CHEER IT

This worship experience allows everyone to be a cheerleader for God's Word. Form groups of three or four. Assign a scripture verse or passage to each group and give groups three or four minutes to develop a cheer based on their passages. Explain that the cheers can be similar to cheers for sporting events but need to clearly communicate the message of the scripture.

This approach works well with Matthew 5:3-12 (the Beatitudes), Matthew 5:13 (the salt of the earth) or with Matthew 5:14-16 (the light of the world).

SCULPTURE IT

Form groups of three or four and assign each group a scripture verse or passage. Have kids develop a living sculpture that symbolizes the message from their scripture. Allow three or four minutes for groups to read their passages and develop their sculptures. Each person must be a part of the sculpture.

When groups are ready, have them take turns reading their scriptures and forming their sculptures. A few verses that work well with this activity are Matthew 6:3-4; 6:6; 6:19-21; 6:22-23; and 6:24.

Music

Music is the language of the soul, and everyone understands it a bit differently. Even without lyrics, there is an undeniable spiritual aspect to music. A throbbing rhythm, a plaintive melody, a celebratory crescendo, intricate counterpoint—all these things can turn our hearts toward God or coax them away. Music makes us vulnerable; it cuts across reason and ties in directly to our emotions. These ideas will help you use music in creative ways to enrich the worship experience.

NEW SONGS AND OLD HYMNS

There is good contemporary Christian music being written that is unfamiliar to many adults. Likewise, most teenagers pay little attention to classic hymns of the faith. How about conducting a New Songs and Old Hymns worship service?

Select two or three adults to present classic hymns and two or three teenagers to present contemporary Christian songs. Have the adults and teenagers work together to plan a service with a teaching format. Invite the leaders to explore the background stories connected with the songs and to present the stories as they're teaching the hymns. These stories often make the songs more meaningful and help worshipers understand how men and women have expressed their faith over the years using notes and words.

Have kids and adults be interspersed in the seating arrangement so each group can catch the enthusiasm of the other. This service can bring generations closer together as they gain a greater appreciation for the music of the faith—old and new.

CLUSTER GROUP-SING

Have worshipers form groups of four to eight. Ask each group to choose its favorite hymn or chorus.

Say: **On my signal, start singing your song with great enthusiasm. Keep singing one verse of your song over and over. Then, when I point to your group, stop singing your song and begin singing "Fairest Lord Jesus"** (or other quiet praise-hymn of your choice) **along with those who are already singing it.**

After about a minute of each group singing a different song, point to one group and lead them in the opening phrase of "Fairest Lord Jesus." Point to another group and have them join you on the second phrase, and so on, until the noisy conglomeration becomes one quiet, prayerful choir.

This worship experience is effective for teenagers and adults alike. As the singing progresses, people understand that no matter how cluttered or chaotic our lives may sometimes seem, everything falls into place when we stand before God.

SING YOUR FEELINGS

Distribute chorus books or hymnals. Invite worshipers to choose a song that expresses where they are in their Christian walk. When people name the song they'd like the group to sing, have them tell why that song is significant at this point in their lives.

TUNE-UPS

Familiar hymns sometimes become mechanical and begin to lose their impact—as if we're singing by rote. Setting the lyrics to a new tune catches worshipers by surprise and brings a new freshness and life to something that's become habitual and overly familiar.

Try singing the lyrics of "Amazing Grace" to the tune of "House of the Rising Sun." Sing the lyrics of "My Jesus, I Love Thee" to the tune of "The Cruel War." Invite kids in your youth group to come up with their own creative combinations.

SCAVENGER ACCOMPANIMENT

Read Psalm 98 responsively and then form groups of three to five kids. Allow five minutes for groups to choose a favorite praise song and come up with "instruments" to accompany it. Limit the instrument hunt to a certain area, such as the church basement or the basement plus the parking lot.

Call time after five minutes and let kids make a joyful noise as they play their instruments and sing!

SONGS IN SIGN

It's always fascinating to express the words of a worship song in sign language. If you don't know someone who can teach signing, encourage kids to create interpretive motions of their own. Form groups for multiverse songs such as "Amen," "The Coloring Song" or "Lord of the Dance" and have each group interpret a different verse.

You'll find these and many other favorite songs in *The Group Songbook* (Group Books).

SIMULTANEOUS SINGING

Songs with identical rhythm patterns can be sung simultaneously, creating a fun, lively effect. "I'm Gonna Sing, Sing, Sing," "Oh, When the Saints Go Marching In," "Swing Low, Sweet Chariot," "This Train Is Bound for Glory" and "Down by the Riverside" are five such songs. These songs are #27 in *The Group Songbook* (Group Books).

Start by singing through all the songs. Then break into groups and layer the songs on each other, adding one song at a time as groups who are already singing keep repeating their songs.

TACTILE SONGS

Passing around a simple prop can add great meaning to a song. Pass a cup of water as you sing "Fill My Cup." Pass a lump of clay as you sing "Change My Heart, Oh God." Pass a flashlight as you sing "Thy Word." Pass a large rock as you sing "Cornerstone." Pass a lighted candle as you sing "Pass It On." Pass crayons as you sing "The Coloring Song." If you really trust your group, pass a squirt gun as you sing "Bubblin' " or "Spring Up, O Well"!

DANCE TO THE MUSIC

Many lively worship songs lend themselves well to a simple circle or folk dance. Have kids put their arms around each other's shoulders and do a simple cross-in-front, cross-behind step as they sing "King of Kings," "Cornerstone" or "Lord of the Dance." Finish off each phrase with a kick and then set the circle or line in motion in the opposite direction for the next phrase.

INTERACTIVE MESSAGES AND SHARING

When you think of planning a creative worship service for the youth group or for the whole congregation, coming up with something fresh for the sermon time can be your biggest challenge. These interactive ideas meet that need by getting worshipers involved in sharing, dialogue and finding encouragement from scripture.

WALKING BY FAITH

Make photocopies of the "Walking by Faith in God's Promises" handout on page 29. You'll need a copy of the handout and a marker for each person.

Open the worship time by reading 2 Corinthians 5:7 and Hebrews 11:1. Ask people to share their personal definitions of faith.

Give each person a handout and a marker. Have worshipers circle one promise from the handout that is really important to them right now. Then have them put the handout on the floor and draw the outline of their foot on it to symbolize "standing" on God's promises. Ask people to tell which verse they chose and why they chose it.

Set up an adjacent area to represent the Jordan River. Use blue and white crepe paper streamers to represent the water. Add small stones to the riverbed—more stones than there are people.

After sharing "foot promises," have the group gather at one side of the Jordan River. Have volunteers take turns reading Joshua 3:8-17 and 4:1-18

Walking by Faith in God's Promises

Circle one promise that is really important to you right now.

If any of you lacks wisdom, he should ask God, who gives generously to all without finding fault, and it will be given to him (James 1:5).

I will instruct you and teach you in the way you should go; I will counsel you and watch over you (Psalm 32:8).

If God is for us, who can be against us? (Romans 8:31b).

Those who sow in tears will reap with songs of joy. He who goes out weeping, carrying seed to sow, will return with songs of joy, carrying sheaves with him (Psalm 126:5-6).

Delight yourself in the Lord and he will give you the desires of your heart. Commit your way to the Lord; trust in him and he will do this: He will make your righteousness shine like the dawn, the justice of your cause like the noonday sun (Psalm 37:4-6).

"For I know the plans I have for you," declares the Lord, "plans to prosper you and not to harm you, plans to give you hope and a future" (Jeremiah 29:11).

And we know that in all things God works for the good of those who love him, who have been called according to his purpose (Romans 8:28).

My grace is sufficient for you, for my power is made perfect in weakness (2 Corinthians 12:9).

Permission to photocopy this handout granted for local church use. Copyright © Group Publishing, Inc., Box 481, Loveland, CO 80539.

aloud. Then say: Stand in the place that represents where you are in your Christian life right now. Are you on the bank just starting to cross? in the middle of the riverbed? or have you crossed over onto the other shore?

After worshipers have taken their places, invite them to say one or two words that describe how they feel in those spots. Then have everyone surround the people who are on the bank or who are just starting to enter the water and offer prayers for them. Next, have everyone surround the people who took places in the middle of the river and pray for them. Last, have everyone surround those who are on the other side and pray for them.

Finally, ask worshipers to return to the riverbed to pick up a stone of remembrance, to remind them that the Lord is with them on their journey of faith.

Close with a song of worship and commitment such as "Father, I Adore You."

DIALOGICAL SERMONS

Dialogical sermons work well in youth-led worship. Choose topics that center on teenagers' concerns, such as:
- What does God's Word say about handling family conflicts?
- How can I know God's will for my life?
- How much of my time and money belong to God?
- What are the dangers of dabbling in the occult?
- How can I be sure that God loves and accepts me?
- Are MTV and secular rock music appropriate for Christian kids?
- How can I share God's love with kids at school?

Consider these formats for dialogical sermons:
- The pastor calls the youth group to the front of the sanctuary where they sit on the front platform like little children often do. Then the pastor and youth group engage in a somewhat-planned dialogue.
- Have a teenager stand at the lectern with the pastor at the pulpit and engage in a give-and-take "debate" sermon. This can be very challenging and not negatively argumentative.

● A panel of teenagers in the front of the sanctuary asks questions of adults in the congregation. Some questions can be planned; others can be spontaneous. Adults may also ask kids probing questions about how faith affects various areas of their lives.

These dialogical sermons are wonderful means of integrating the kids and their thought processes, concerns and successes into the congregation as a whole.

FIVE-MINUTE REPORTS

When your youth group attends a special event, invite kids to give the sermon the following Sunday in a series of three- to five-minute reports. Each report can be given by a different person on a different aspect of the event. Kids might report on a day's theme, quotes from the speakers, and highlights of the event. They can also thank the congregation for helping them raise the funds to attend. This group sermon helps the congregation receive a bit of the event's flavor—the enthusiasm, the spiritual high and the fun.

If some kids prefer not to participate in the group sermon, print quotations from them in the day's worship folder. Consider creating a custom-made folder with a photograph of the event's site along with quotes from participants.

SHINING STARS

Distribute paper and pencils and have participants draw a large, five-pointed star on their papers. Read aloud Philippians 2:12-15 and then give the following instructions: **On the five points of your star, write these five things:**

- **your name,**
- **a time when you shined,**
- **a time when you felt God very near,**
- **a time you were truly a servant of God and**
- **a time you needed more light.**

After each instruction, allow a few moments for writing. Then have worshipers form "constellations" of three or four to share what they wrote. When worshipers in each constellation have finished sharing, invite them to tape their stars to a wall. Gather everyone in front of the starry wall to sing "Shine, Jesus, Shine" or "This Little Light of Mine."

Distribute more paper and have participants return to their seats and draw a second star. Give these instructions, pausing after each one:

- **On the top point of your star draw a head and write ways you stay connected to Christ.**
- **On the two side points draw two hands and write the names of two people you'd like to reach out to.**
- **On the bottom two points draw two feet and write two personal goals you'd like to accomplish in your journey of faith during the coming year.**

Have participants form new constellations of three or four and share what they wrote. As the sharing draws to a close, say: **Turn your paper over and write these scripture references on the back of the points: Genesis 26:4; Psalm 147:1-5; Psalm 148:1-6; 1 Corinthians 15:41-44; and Revelation 22:16. Read one scripture each night for the next five nights. Wonder about the "points" and let God speak to you.**

Have everyone stand in the shape of a star and hold hands. Invite each person to pray, "Jesus, shine through me when I'm ..." Close with a group hug.

PRAISING GOD

As worshipers gather, hand out the following list and ask each person to prepare one item from the list to share with the group. Play soft worship music as people prepare.

- Read a Bible passage and tell how or when it has encouraged you.

- Choose a song and tell why it's meaningful to you. If the song is familiar, we'll sing it together.

- Tell about a time when praising God was helpful in your life.

- Tell about a difficult situation you're facing that makes it hard for you to praise God. The group will pray for you.

- Declare God's goodness in your life by sharing an answer to prayer or telling how God is working in your life.

- Share an insight about praise.

Permission to photocopy this box granted for local church use.
Copyright © Group Publishing, Inc., Box 481, Loveland CO 80539.

Begin the worship time by reading 1 Timothy 4:9-10. Then have worshipers share what they've prepared. Close the worship time with a song chosen by one of the worshipers or with a prayer.

ME-TOO SHARING

Sharing times can unintentionally focus on "I'll top your story" rather than on "I understand and empathize with what you've said." Me-too sharing helps the latter happen. Each time someone shares, at least three others tell why they agree with that request or why they want to pray that also.

Examples of me-too responses are "I want courage to build closeness at home, too, because it's hard to keep my temper around younger siblings"; "I want to appreciate normal life more, too"; "I often whine about what's *not* going on rather than noticing the good things God is already giving me" and "I agree that we need Frank's encouraging words because he reminds us that God loves us personally."

Effective topics for me-too sharing include:
- how I want to serve God (Romans 12:1),
- how I want to open myself to God's transforming power (Romans 12:2),

- why I'm worth loving and being loved (Romans 12:3-6),
- the good I see in each member of this group (Romans 12:7-8) and
- how we can build love here (Romans 12:9-21).

PASS-AROUND PROP

Any youth leader knows how hard it is to get kids to pay attention to and cherish what's being said by each person. A prop can be a helpful tool in achieving this goal because only the person holding it can speak. A flashlight works well for this. Darken the room and have kids hold the flashlight on their faces or on their Bibles while they talk. The dim room seems to free kids to speak more openly, and passing the flashlight helps them focus on the discussion. Three good rules for prop-passing are:

- Only the person who's holding the prop may speak.
- No one can request the prop next until the current holder stops talking.
- The prop must go to three other people before it comes back to the current speaker.

Any worship topic or scripture works well with pass-around props. Here are some other effective prop ideas:

- theme-related items such as a cup of water for Mark 9:41 or a book of matches for Daniel 3,
- a ball of yarn (Have kids hold on to a strand of yarn as they pass the ball along. This idea is so old that it's new to today's kids!),
- an egg timer (it keeps any one person from talking too long) and
- a poster that kids have created together for the worship experience.

"S'NOW" SHARING

Sometimes kids and leaders get locked into thinking that worship needs to include long sermon-type sharing about dramatic transformations. Not so! Kids need to know that worship can help them:

● discover how faith connects to everyday life,

● find joy and comfort in sharing their faith with friends, and

● understand that sharing can be significant even if it isn't dramatic or lengthy.

"S'NOW" (rhymes with how) sharing helps accomplish these goals. This kind of sharing is "S"hort and focuses on what's happening right NOW. Kids talk for no more than a minute about a way God has helped them in the present month. Encourage them to focus on present obedience rather than past disobedience; this makes it more appealing to obey God than to have a sinful past. Kids can share things such as the words God gave them to turn down a drinking encounter or a friendship that grew when they reached out to someone new. In this way they celebrate God's involvement in the details of life.

BREAD TALKS

Bread talks are a great way to get kids in a youth group to share personal concerns with each other. Have kids sit in a circle and pass around a loaf of shepherd's bread. Each person breaks off a piece of the bread and shares a prayer concern. The kids can keep sharing concerns and passing the bread around the circle as long as the loaf of bread holds out!

Just a few minutes of this type of sharing creates a sense of caring community in a youth group. It's great to follow the bread talks with a Bible study that addresses kids' needs and then close with a circle of prayer.

FIRESIDE SHARING

Build a bonfire and gather worshipers in a circle around it. Place a pile of twigs a few feet from the fire. Invite worshipers to share how God has been working in their lives. After each person shares, have him or her throw a twig onto the fire. This simple sharing service works well in a retreat setting.

FLOATING LIGHTS

This very moving service takes place in the late evening by a river. For each worshiper you'll need an emergency or votive candle pressed into the center of a 5-inch square of rigid foam insulation. The insulation allows the candles to float.

Gather by the shore of a river. Have volunteers read the following passages about light: Genesis 1:3; Psalm 27:1; Psalm 89:15; Isaiah 9:2; Matthew 5:14-16; John 1:1-5; John 8:12; Ephesians 5:8; and 1 John 1:5-7. Light one candle and then light the readers' candles just before each one reads. After all the passages have been read, pass the light to worshipers whose candles haven't yet been lit.

When all the candles have been lit, have worshipers take turns sharing about someone they would like to be a light to and someone who has been a light in their lives. After worshipers share, have them float their candles on the water and push them into the current. As the string of lights goes floating down the river, sing "Pass It On."

Send someone to retrieve the candles after the service closes.

GOD'S HAND ON YOU

As kids come in the door, have them each use ink to put a thumbprint on a slip of paper. Write kids' initials very lightly on the back of their thumbprints. Display all the thumbprints on a table and give kids one minute to find their own without peeking at the initials. Don't be surprised if the success rate isn't too high!

Say: **We're all uniquely made by God, and we each reflect God's image in our own special way. In some ways we're so unique that we don't even know ourselves too well!**

Form a circle. Have volunteers read aloud Psalm 139:1-16 and Matthew 10:30-31.

Say: **Pull out a strand of hair and give it to a person sitting next to you. Tell that person how it feels to know that God knows everything about you. Then look up and read Isaiah 64:8 together.**

Allow about two minutes for sharing. Then call on someone to sit in the center of the circle. Read Isaiah 64:8, inserting that person's name: (Name) **is the clay, you are the potter;** (name) **is the work of your hand.**

Then say: **We know that God's hand is on** (name) **because...**

Encourage several people to finish the sentence with words of affirmation. Do this with each person in the circle. Close the sharing with a group hug.

SPECIAL SEASONS

At times you'd like to address church and national holidays in your worship time without developing an entire creative worship service. These quick ideas will enhance your worship times and help your group learn from and enjoy the significance of several special days.

PALM BRANCHES

On special occasions such as Palm Sunday, Easter and times when you celebrate in your local congregation, give worshipers "palm branches" to wave as you sing praise songs. Lengths of ribbon looped through plastic rings make colorful palm branches you can use again and again. Or simply give each person a crepe paper streamer.

THE CRUCIFIXION

Do a dramatic reading of the Crucifixion story with your congregation. Divide the sanctuary into sections and assign a leader and specific roles to each section. Paraphrase Matthew 26:47–27:50, assigning solo parts to people who are planted throughout the congregation and choral readings to various sections of the congregation. For instance, one section of the congregation might represent the angry, restless crowd while another section might represent Jesus' accusers. Print the reading in a worship folder.

Arrange for live or taped music or a combination of both to introduce the reading and provide a background for it. Set the mood by darkening the sanctuary, allowing just enough light so people can read.

EASTER MARCH

Lead your group in a triumphal march around your church or neighborhood to celebrate Christ's triumph over death. Begin the march with a reading of 2 Corinthians 2:14-17. Sing lively songs of Jesus' victory and lordship, accompanied by tambourines and clapping.

ASCENSION DAY HIKE

Celebrate Ascension Day with a walk or "car hike." Plan your route with six stops at parks or quiet, shady places. Make your last stop at the top of a hill. Choose six readers and give them each one of the following scripture references: (1) Matthew 28:8-10; (2) Luke 24:13-27; (3) Luke 24:28-35; (4) Luke 24:36-49; (5) John 20:24-29; and (6) Luke 24:50-52. Make sure the readers bring their Bibles along.

Sing praise songs as you begin your walk. At the first stop, call on the first reader to read his or her passage aloud. Sing on your way to the second stop and then have the second passage read. Continue in this manner until the last passage is read at the top of a hill. As Jesus' ascension is described, release a few helium balloons and watch them until they disappear from sight—just as Jesus' disciples watched. Read Jesus' words from Matthew 28:18-20 as a benediction.

MEMORIAL DAY

The week prior to Memorial Day, take your group on a field trip to a cemetery where deceased church members are buried. Have kids use newsprint and pencils to do rubbings of the gravestones of deceased church members and other gravestones with interesting inscriptions.

Display the rubbings in the front of the sanctuary. Invite worshipers to share positive memories of the people whose gravestones are represented and stories of how those people influenced others for Christ. Have the congregation read Hebrews 12:1-2 in unison to close the service.

INDEPENDENCE DAY

On this special day as our country celebrates its independence, celebrate your *dependence* on God by creating a Declaration of Dependence. Form groups of four to six and have each group write its own declaration, incorporating scriptures that encourage us to rely on God for all our needs.

After a few minutes of writing time, bring everyone together and have groups present their declarations. Sing a verse of a patriotic hymn between the groups' presentations.

BANNER DAYS

If your group enjoys art projects, invite kids to work together on banners to represent various holidays and special days in the church calendar. Encourage kids to include in their banners symbols that have personal meaning for them. Have group members present their banners to the congregation along with scripture readings and personal sharing that explain the banners' significance.

CREATIVE WORSHIP WORKSHEET

Use this worksheet to develop your own creative worship services with resources from the "Creative Worship Ingredients" section.

What is the theme of the service?

Who and how many will attend?

How can you draw worshipers into the theme?

What atmosphere do you want to create?

What scriptures relate to the theme?

What message from God is contained in the scriptures?

How can worshipers experience the scriptures?

What music relates to the scriptures?

How will the music be presented?

When and how will worshipers pray?

When and how will worshipers encourage and share with each other?

How will the worship experience come to a close?

Permission to photocopy this handout granted for local church use. Copyright © Group Publishing, Inc., Box 481, Loveland, CO 80539.

Part Two

CREATIVE SKITS

by Paul Lessard

Use these lively, thought-provoking skits to
drive home important spiritual truths to your
youth group or congregation.

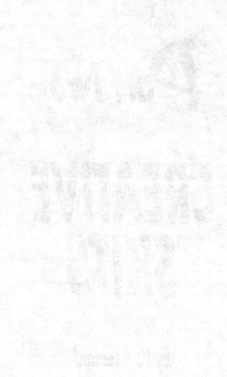

WHAT DO YOU CALL THIS PLACE?

THEME: The church

SCRIPTURE: And let us consider how we may spur one another on toward love and good deeds (Hebrews 10:24).

SYNOPSIS: People with different life ailments come to a "hospital" hoping it has room. This illustrates how the church needs to respond to hurting people.

CHARACTERS:
Nurse—a warm, kind, take-charge person
Ms. York—a businesswoman
Sam Iam—a tough construction worker
Mr. Rap—a rapper, bouncy, never still
Winnie—a desperate single-mom

PROPS: a table and six chairs

[The scene opens with the nurse sitting at a table with one chair facing her. The patients are sitting in a row facing the congregation, as if in a waiting room. They should be in character as they sit, with Ms. York very businesslike, Sam slouching and looking awkward, Mr. Rap humming and thumping, and Winnie looking quite sad and occasionally wiping her eyes. Be careful not to let their movements upstage the nurse. After each interview, characters exit the stage opposite of where they were sitting.]

NURSE: *(looking up from her papers)* Ms. York, please. *(Ms. York sits down across from the nurse.)*

NURSE: *(smiles)* It says here that you're a businesswoman.

MS. YORK: *(very businesslike)* That is correct.

NURSE: Well, we have many businesspeople come to us. What can we do for you?

MS. YORK: *(briskly)* I've been having some trouble with my heart. It feels terrible and I don't know what to do. Actually, I've had this problem as long as I can remember. It's just become more pronounced lately.

NURSE: Have you tried success at work?

MS. YORK: Oh yes. And I've done very well. I am well-respected in my field and make plenty of money. I thought that all those things would make my heart better, not worse. But... *(voice trails off)*

NURSE: It sounds to me like you have a hole in your heart. Do you feel empty inside?

MS. YORK: *(relieved that someone understands)* That is exactly how I feel. Can you help me?

NURSE: Sure we can. We can introduce you to the Doctor. He takes care of this kind of thing all the time. He'll fix that hole and fill the emptiness. Just go through that door and they'll take care of you.
(Ms. York smiles and exits.)

NURSE: Mr. Iam *(pronounced "I am")*, please.

SAM: *(as he walks over and sits down)* Just call me Sam.

NURSE: How can we help you, Sam Iam?

SAM: *(boisterous)* All the time at work, see, on the job, I got these guys twisting my arm *(holds out his arm and rubs it)* to do things I don't wanna do. I'm tired of livin' like this and wondered if you guys could help me have more backbone to stand up for what I believe in. Can you guys help me with this? This ain't too much to ask, is it?

NURSE: Not at all, Sam. We can help you have more backbone and stronger arms so you can help other people, too.

SAM: Aw, that's great.

NURSE: Just go through that door over there and they will help you.

SAM: *(as he leaves)* This is such a relief. I just hope I don't have to wear one of those gowns that's open at the back.

NURSE: Mr. Rap, please.
(Mr. Rap dances his way over to the nurse and sits down.)

MR. RAP: Yo, nurse, I hope you can help me!

NURSE: *(clearing her throat and trying to be hip but failing)* Yo, Mr. Rap, we'll sure try. Mr. Rap, it says here that you're having trouble with your hearing. Is this true?

MR. RAP: *(in rap style)* I've been listening to the world,
And I hear it quite fine,
But when it comes to hearing truth,
I'm deaf all the time.
Te-Tell me where can I go
And what I need to do
To get this wax removed
So I can hear what's true.

NURSE: We can help you with that. In fact, not only can we help your hearing become better, we can introduce you to the Doctor who can give you a new mind as well. *(smiles sweetly at him)*

MR. RAP: A new mind? Check this out! This is a serious place you got here!

NURSE: Just dance on over there through that door, and they can help you. *(Mr. Rap dances off.)*

NURSE: *(looks up at the last remaining patient)* Winnie? *(Winnie walks over but doesn't sit down)* Please have a seat. Winnie, it says here you are a single mother of two kids and you were just laid off at work. *(tenderly)* Tell me, where does it hurt?

WINNIE: *(broken up)* All over. I've been badly beaten by life, I think my heart is broken and I just don't know where to turn anymore. *(hesitantly)* Do you think you could help me?

NURSE: *(gently)* We most certainly can. To start with, the Doctor can give you a new heart. And then we'll surround you with love and try to give you and your family the support and encouragement you need.

WINNIE: *(afraid to ask)* Do ... do you have room for me then?

NURSE: Of course. And we have room for your children as well.

WINNIE: *(very grateful)* Thank you so much. You don't know how it feels to get a second chance. *(as she gets up to leave)* You've been so kind and caring, what do you call this place?

NURSE: *(smiles)* We call it the church. *(As Winnie walks off, the nurse turns to the congregation and says ...)* Next? *(freeze)*

TOOTH DECAY

THEME: Sin

SCRIPTURE: Count yourselves dead to sin but alive to God in Christ Jesus. Therefore do not let sin reign in your mortal body so that you obey its evil desires (Romans 6:11-12).

SYNOPSIS: Four teeth discuss how plaque is like sin.

CHARACTERS: four people to be teeth, each with a unique voice; Tooth #2 has the deep voice of a wisdom tooth; two workpeople to floss and clean teeth

PROPS: four tooth costumes made of pillowcases with holes cut out for faces, rope for floss and a big red tongue made of soft plastic foam made to be manipulated by a person's arm

(The scene opens with four teeth humming and whistling. The teeth should stand behind something so their legs can't be seen.)

TOOTH #1: That was a good meal, wasn't it?

TOOTH #4: It was great!

TOOTH #3: I love working on steamed broccoli. It's crunchy and firm but not **too** hard.

TOOTH #4: If it's not steamed too long.
(While they're talking, the two workpeople walk over and put the rope around Tooth #1 and start flossing. Tooth #1 moves as if getting a good back rub.)

TOOTH #1: Aaahhh, that feels great! I'm gonna tell ya, a good stiff brushing with a fluoride toothpaste, that is, of course, recommended by nine out of 10 dentists, and a quick after-dinner floss, and I feel like a new tooth!
(Workpeople keep flossing, moving down the row of teeth.)

TOOTH #2: You know, our owner takes good care of us.

TOOTH #3: Yes, she does. She keeps us looking nice and white.

TOOTH #4: Except when she eats blueberries.
(All teeth laugh like it's the funniest thing they've heard)

TOOTH #2: It's too bad she doesn't take as much care of the rest of herself.

TOOTH #1: What d'ya mean?

TOOTH #2: Well, if she ignores us and doesn't keep us clean, we start to decay. *(All shudder.)* And even though everything **seems** fine, one day she'll wake up and we'll be aching and causing her a lot of pain. Then she may even lose us.

TOOTH #3: Can we change the subject. I . . .

TOOTH #1: What are you tryin' to say?

TOOTH #2: Well, it's the same with her soul. If she doesn't take care of it and treat it right, it will start to decay. You see, sin creeps in like plaque *(All shudder and turn away)* and eats away. If she's not careful, she may lose her soul!

ALL: *(in awe)* Wow. That's serious stuff!

TOOTH #4: Now we know why they call you a wisdom tooth!
(Workpeople finish and leave.)

TOOTH #1: Hey guys, it looks like she's finished.

TOOTH #3: Oh no—now she's gonna feel how clean we are!
Brace yourselves!
(A big tongue comes up and feels the tops and sides of all the teeth. They giggle and laugh as they are poked and prodded.)
(freeze)

THE NEW CONDENSED BIBLE

THEME: God's truth

SCRIPTURE: God's word is alive and working and is sharper than a double-edged sword (Hebrews 4:12).

SYNOPSIS: In a pitch for a new version of the Bible, a salesperson inadvertently shows us how we avoid passages of scripture that we find convicting.

CHARACTER: a fast-talking, overly genuine salesperson who smiles continuously

PROPS: a very tiny book and an old book that can be ripped up

(The scene opens with the salesperson holding the old book. The tiny book should be in his pocket. As the salesperson talks about what has been taken out of the Bible, he starts ripping pages out of the old book and tossing them over his shoulder. The entire time he's smiling and enthusiastic.)

SALESPERSON: Hello! Are you tired of those **other** versions of the Bible? You know, the versions that make you feel uncomfortable, uneasy, guilty and maybe even a little itchy when you read them? Me too! I've had it up to here with "turn or burn" and "doom and gloom." But now you don't have to put up with a Bible that doesn't match up with how you live. Yes, there **is** a better Bible available and if you dial 1-800-77BIBLE before midnight tonight, you too can have your own copy of the New Condensed Bible.

Yes, this is the Bible that takes out all the uncomfortable stuff and leaves just the promises and the positive thinking. *(begins to rip pages out of the old book)* Tired of reading about giving and what to do with your money? *(rip)* It's all gone. Does the stuff about sexuality and morals make you feel bad about how you've been living? *(rip)* You won't find it here! In fact, any verse, word or letter that our editors found even remotely offending has been taken completely out.

What **will** you find in the New Condensed Bible? You'll discover all the best, happiest and most fun stuff boiled down to a single line or two. For example, in other versions you'd read in the book of Philippians *(opens what's left of the old book)* "Do not be anxious about anything, but in everything, by prayer and petition, with thanksgiving, present your requests to God." *(pulls out the tiny book)* In the New Condensed Bible it simply reads "Don't worry...be happy!"

Yes, dial 1-800-77BIBLE before midnight tonight and order the New Condensed Bible. Let it bring the fun back into your Bible reading. You'll find it light to hold, quick to read and easy to forget. *(big smile)* The New Condensed Bible. It's the perfect Bible for people who think they're already perfect!
(freeze)

THE CLEAN-UP

THEME: Anger

SCRIPTURE: If you are offering your gift at the altar and there remember that your brother has something against you, leave your gift there in front of the altar. First go and be reconciled to your brother; then come and offer your gift (Matthew 5:23-24).

SYNOPSIS: A husband and wife are involved in a conversation where he thinks she is admitting her anger, when she's really complaining about cleaning the oven. We learn how letting an oven get dirty is a lot like how our anger builds up.

CHARACTERS:
Narrator
Eunice—a frustrated wife
Ed—a well-meaning but not too "with-it" husband

PROPS: a chair, a newspaper, rubber gloves and a bottle of spray cleaner

(The scene opens with Ed sitting in a chair and reading a newspaper. Eunice is on the other side of the stage miming cleaning an oven. The set suggests that they're in two different rooms.)

NARRATOR: Scripture tells us to be reconciled with those who have hurt us. It's plain that as God's people, we are to deal honestly with our anger and live holy lives. This is not unlike a woman who was cleaning her oven ...

EUNICE: That's it! I've had it. This oven is so dirty I'll never get it clean. *(raising her voice)* This whole thing has gotten out of hand!

ED: *(absently)* What's that, Eunice?

EUNICE: *(yelling)* I said, "This whole thing has gotten out of hand!"

ED: *(yelling)* What are you talking about?

EUNICE: *(yelling)* My oven!

ED: *(crumples newspaper in his lap, rather confused)* Her cousin? *(realization dawning)* Eunice has finally identified the reason she's so frustrated—she's **angry** with her cousin! *(yelling)* What do you mean when you say, "This whole thing has gotten out of hand?"

EUNICE: *(to herself)* This oven will never come clean in my lifetime. *(yelling)* I mean it has gotten very bad. I guess I thought by ignoring it, it would just go away.

ED: *(to himself)* This is incredible! Eunice is admitting she let her anger grow. *(yelling)* So do I hear you saying you're responsible for the problem?

EUNICE: *(yelling)* Of course, it's totally my fault. *(sarcastically, rolling her eyes and talking to herself)* No one else uses the oven around here. *(yelling)* I just let things build up. *(to herself)* It may take dynamite to get the crud out of this thing.

ED: *(to himself)* Amazing! She admits she let things build up. I wonder if I should call her cousin and ask her to come over so Eunice can apologize. No, that's moving too fast. *(yelling)* Honey, is there anything I can do to help?

EUNICE: *(yelling)* No, I'm just going to have to face it on my own. I think if I scrape away at it, I can remove it layer by layer. *(to herself)* I think I need a hammer and chisel.

ED: *(to himself)* She wants to remove it layer by layer. Wow— she really wants to deal with her anger! *(yelling)* What made you aware of the problem?

EUNICE: *(to herself)* Brother, you can tell he doesn't help out in the kitchen very often. *(yelling)* I just opened the door and I couldn't help but see the black stuff built up. I can't ignore it anymore.

ED: *(full of pride)* That's my Eunice! She opened the door to her heart, saw the blackness of sin and was unable to ignore her anger any longer. And now she's going to do something about it. *(yelling)* Honey, I want you to know I support you in this matter and I'm very proud of you!

EUNICE: *(sits up and wipes her hand across her brow, then speaks quizzically)* He's proud of me? If he's proud of me for cleaning the oven, I wonder how he'd feel if I cleaned the garage?
(freeze)

LAMPS 'R' US

THEME: God's Word
SCRIPTURE: Your word is a lamp to my feet and a light for my path (Psalm 119:105).

SYNOPSIS: A man goes into a shop to buy a Bible lamp. He wants to make sure that the lamps they sell will work in all of life's situations.

CHARACTER:
   Anne—a salesperson, perky and eager to help
   Mark—well-meaning but melodramatic

PROPS: a telephone; a table; Bibles of all sizes, shapes and versions; two adhesive bandages; a cloth; a pocket New Testament and a bag

(The scene opens with Anne on the phone. The table is piled full of Bibles. Mark enters and waits patiently. The two adhesive bandages should be placed across his nose like a big X.)

ANNE: *(answers the phone)* Lamps 'R' Us—we light up your life! Can I help you? *(pause)* We're open until 5:30. *(pause)* You're welcome, goodbye. *(looks up at Mark)* Can I help you, sir?

MARK: Yes, I'm looking for a good light. It seems like the world is getting darker and darker, and I've been having trouble finding my way. *(points to his nose)* I keep walking into trees, buildings and stuff like that.

ANNE: I'm sure I can help you. We have many quality lamps here at Lamps 'R' Us.

MARK: What brand names do you carry?

ANNE: Oh, we only carry one brand because we've found that we couldn't guarantee the quality of the other brands. Their lights kept dying out. *(shakes her head)* You don't want an unreliable light, do you? *(picks up a Bible and begins to clean it with a cloth)*

MARK: *(shudders at the thought)* No ma'am! What brand do you carry then?

ANNE: We carry the Bible lamp. It's been a lamp to people and a light for their paths for hundreds of years. It's got a proven track record—it's shined in the dark for a long time.

MARK: *(firmly)* That sounds like the kind of light I'm looking for. I need a light that's big enough to help me see where I'm going when the storm clouds of life make it dark and treacherous out there. What sizes do you have?

ANNE: Well, as you can see, they come in all sizes. But you should know that all of our lamps throw the same amount of light, regardless of size.

MARK: *(picking up the pocket New Testament)* Even the little pocket size?

ANNE: Any size can blind you with its light if you're not careful.

MARK: Can your lamps throw light into the deepest, blackest pit of despair?

ANNE: They can.
(Tempo of the lines should start to pick up.)

MARK: *(increasingly intense)* When this life threatens to overwhelm me, when the pain gets too much to bear, when all that I've worked for turns to ashes, will your lamps still shine?

ANNE: Guaranteed!

MARK: *(quickly)* When persistent, persnickety people purposely exert peer pressure, proposing perplexing, pernicious plans, **will these lamps clearly show me which way to go?**

ANNE: Undoubtedly!

MARK: *(with great emotion)* When the woman I've loved ...

ANNE: *(patience wearing thin, interrupting)* Listen, are you going to buy a lamp or not?

MARK: *(clears his throat and returns to a normal tone of voice)* Yes, please. I'll take two. One pocket size and one full size. *(to himself as she bags the Bibles)* It feels good to know that as I travel the highways and byways of life, I'll finally have a good and dependable light.

ANNE: *(as she bags the Bibles)* I think you'll find that whatever you encounter in life, one of our Bible lamps will shed light on the issue and show you which way to go. Here you are, sir.

MARK: Thank you very much. I can't wait to try it out. *(turns to leave)*

ANNE: If you don't mind me asking, sir, what do you do for a living?

MARK: I write soap operas. I used to write for "The Edge of Darkness," but now I write for "Guiding Light." *(walks off stage)*

ANNE: *(picks up the phone)* Lamps 'R' Us—we light up your life! Can I help you?
(freeze)

TRUST ME

THEME: Trust
SCRIPTURE: Trust in the Lord with all your heart and lean not on your own understanding (Proverbs 3:5).

SYNOPSIS: While getting her hair styled, a woman learns a lesson about trust.

CHARACTERS:
Narrator
Sid—the hairdresser, professional, not very talkative
Kelly—the "hairdressee," somewhat paranoid

PROPS: a stool, a sheet, scissors, a comb and hairspray

(The scene opens with Kelly already on the stool and Sid putting the sheet around her neck. Sid is all business and a man of few words. He should always be working, consumed by his craft, almost oblivious to Kelly. Kelly's hair should be teased and quite wild so that as Sid works, he is in fact smoothing it down and making it look better.)

NARRATOR: When we give ourselves to God, he asks that we trust him completely to change and remake us as he sees fit. Sometimes we pull back and our actions end up denying that we really do trust him. That is not unlike the woman who went to her hairdresser . . .

KELLY: . . . so I said to him if that's how you feel, then I'm outta here! Do you think I was too hard on him, Sid?

SID: No.

KELLY: So you're probably wondering what I want done to my hair this time.

SID: Yes.

KELLY: I want something new and radical. Understand? You're the best in town, so I'm putting myself into your hands, Sid. You have my complete trust. Do what you think is best.

SID: Great.
(Sid starts using the scissors behind her head, making very loud noises like he's cutting lots of hair.)

KELLY: *(nervous)* Whoa, how much are you cutting back there? I mean, that didn't sound too good. Is everything okay?

SID: Fine.

KELLY: I want you to know I trust you completely, Sid. I believe you can make me look better...Why are you working on the back so much?

SID: *(pushing the side of her head to tilt it)* Tilt your head, please.

KELLY: *(panicked)* Why?

SID: *(working on the side, making a big cutting sound with the scissors)* Ummm ...

KELLY: *(sits up)* What? Did you cut too much? Am I gonna look bad? *(nervously, to herself)* I knew this was going to be a mistake. *(fakey)* Sid, you're the best hairdresser in town, I'm sure you'll do a great job—right?

SID: Right. *(pushing her head forward)* Tilt forward, please.

KELLY: *(talking with her chin on her chest)* Sid, do you know what you want my hair to look like?

SID: Yes.

KELLY: *(trying to convince herself)* And it **will** be good. It'll be **great.** People will say, "Hey, who cut your hair?" And I'll say, "Sid cut my hair—doesn't it look wonderful?" *(trying to send a message to Sid)* And the people will say, "Oh, Kelly, it **does** look wonderful. That Sid, what a hairdresser he is." Do people say that about you, Sid?

SID: Don't know. *(starts working on the top of her head with a comb and hairspray)*

KELLY: *(nervously)* Listen, Sid, could I see a mirror just for a second? You know—just to see how great it's looking?

SID: *(puts his arms down, turns Kelly to face him and looks her straight in the eye)* Kelly, trust me. *(turns her back around and continues on the top of her head)*

KELLY: *(earnestly)* Sid, I do trust you! What makes you think I don't?
(freeze)

THE OIL SLICK

THEME: Character

SCRIPTURE: Your righteousness is everlasting and your law is true. Trouble and distress have come upon me, but your commands are my delight. Your statutes are forever right; give me understanding that I may live (Psalm 119:142-144).

SYNOPSIS: A teenager's response to bad road conditions reveals his immaturity as a driver. In the same way, our true character is revealed in the pressure points of life.

CHARACTERS:
Randy and Mandy—two teenagers
five people to be a car—two to act as reclining seats, two to act as windshield wipers, and one to act as pop-up headlights

Narrator

PROPS: materials to sound an off-stage crash

(The scene opens with five people positioned as parts of a car. Mandy is sitting in the lap of the person who's the driver's seat. Randy walks by and sees the car. He runs over enthusiastically.)

RANDY: Wow! Is this your car?

MANDY: It sure is. Do you wanna go for a ride, Randy?

RANDY: I'd love to! *(an idea dawns)* Hey, Mandy, could I drive?

MANDY: Well, I don't know ... Have you taken driver's ed?

RANDY: Not really, but I **do** know how to drive. *(pleadingly)* I'll be really careful—I promise!

MANDY: Well, okay—but take it easy.
(She slides over onto the lap of another "seat." Randy sits in the lap of the person who's the driver's seat and checks out the car.)

RANDY: This car is incredible! Check out these windshield wipers!
(The windshield wiper people move their arms, imitating the motion of windshield wipers.)

MANDY: And it has reclining seats.
(Both of the "seats" go back.)

RANDY: And pop-up headlights!
(The headlight person lifts both hands to be the pop-up headlights. Randy starts the car and all the car parts begin to vibrate and hum.)

RANDY: This car is really quiet! Let's see what it can do on the highway. *(He mimes pulling into traffic.)*

MANDY: Please be careful . . .

RANDY: Hey, I'm a great driver. Don't worry. *(yelling)* Hey! Drive it or park it! I think I'm gonna pass this car.

MANDY: Randy, you're going too fast.

RANDY: Listen, I'm in control.

MANDY: But if you haven't been driving very long … Oh no! Look out for the oil on the road!

(All the car parts screech.)

RANDY: Oh no!

(Arrange an off-stage crash. People who are the car assume a smashed position. There's a pause of stunned silence)

RANDY: *(quietly)* Are you okay?

MANDY: I think so. How 'bout you?

RANDY: I'm okay. What happened?

MANDY: You slammed on the brakes—that's the wrong thing to do when you hit something slippery on the road.

RANDY: I didn't know that—it seemed the natural thing to do.

MANDY: In this kind of a crisis you find out how good you really are because you don't have time to think—you just react.

RANDY: *(surveys the damage)* Sorry about your car.

MANDY: Me too. I guess I'll just have to take it to some kind of **body** shop.

(Freeze)

NARRATOR: The same principle is true in our Christian lives. If our faith is shallow and superficial, the crises of life will throw us into a spin. But if our faith is rooted in God's Word, the pressures we face will reveal God's strength within us.

REASON TO PARTY

THEME: Christmas

SCRIPTURE: He came to that which was his own, but his own did not receive him (John 1:11).

SYNOPSIS: A girl is forgotten at her own birthday party.

CHARACTERS:
Amy—the birthday girl, as small as possible, but old enough to play the part
various kids—Ben, Brady, Nathan, Matthew, Christopher, Chantell, Brittany, Isaac
(The speaking parts can be combined to use fewer kids.)
Narrator

PROPS: a table and several gifts loosely wrapped in plenty of wrapping paper

(The scene opens with Amy sitting on a table with the other kids all around her. Everyone should be talking and laughing until Amy starts to talk. When the kids open the gifts, there should be such a flurry of activity that no one really understands what's happening until everyone leaves and Amy is left completely covered with wrapping paper.)

AMY: *(all smiles)* Hey, you guys—thanks for coming to my birthday party!

BEN: What about the presents?

AMY: Thank you all for the birthday presents.

BRADY: No, he means when are you going to open the presents?

BOYS: *(each take a phrase and repeat it)* Open them now! Yeah, now! Let's see what you got!

GIRLS: *(each take a phrase and repeat it)* After the games! Let's play first! I gave her the best present!

AMY: I think . . . I'd like to play games first.

BOYS: Aw—no way!

GIRLS: Yeah, let's play!

NATHAN: Can you open one present now?

MATTHEW: Just one, please?

AMY: Well, all right.

ALL: Pick mine! Open that one! Hurry up—we want to see what you got!

AMY: *(picking up a gift)* I think I'll open this one. *(begins to tear the paper off and continues unwrapping as the following conversation unfolds)*

CHRISTOPHER: *(unclear on the concept but trying to be helpful)* I'll open this one.

CHANTELL: Hey, you can't open her presents.

BEN: If he's gonna open a present, I'm gonna open one, too!

BRITTANY: I'll open this one.

ALL: I've got this one! Give me that one.
(Pandemonium ensues as they each open a present. They should all be blocking Amy so one of the kids can arrange all the boxes and paper to cover her up. This should only take about 30 seconds and needs to be well-rehearsed. Group Publishing will pay for all the wrapping paper you use, just send in your receipts . . . just kidding!)

BRADY: This is cool—I got a game!

BRITTANY: Look at this—a Prom Barbie!

ISAAC: *(standing at the side)* Wow, a new Nintendo game. Why don't you guys come over to my place and we'll all play Nintendo?

ALL: Yeah! Great idea! That'd be fun! Let's play! This is the best party I've ever been to!
(They all run off stage, laughing and talking, leaving Amy covered in wrapping paper and boxes. Her feet should be hanging down from the table. Slowly, she moves and lets the wrappings fall off her. She slides off the table, stands and looks around.)

AMY: *(sadly)* I don't think they really cared that it was my birthday. They just wanted a reason to party. *(begins to pick up the mess, then freezes)*

NARRATOR: As we celebrate this season, let's remember that Christmas is **not** just another reason to party.

THE KID WITH BOXER SHORTS ON HIS HEAD

THEME: Peer pressure

SCRIPTURE: Do not conform any longer to the pattern of this world, but be transformed by the renewing of your mind. Then you will be able to test and approve what God's will is—his good, pleasing and perfect will (Romans 12:2).

SYNOPSIS: A high schooler makes himself look ridiculous in an effort to be accepted by his friends.

CHARACTERS:
  Darryl—a high school kid, really enthusiastic and upbeat
  Mom
  Dad
  Two of Darryl's friends

PROPS: sofa or two chairs, newspaper, boxer shorts, something to simulate the sound of a doorbell, and socks

[The scene opens with Mom and Dad reading the newspaper.]

DAD: My word, Mother, it says here that last month over 300 pigs died from colorblindness.

MOM: *(absently)* That's interesting. Does it say why?

DAD: Nope, but scientists are working to perfect a color-correction contact lens for them.

MOM: *(putting down her handwork)* Oh, Herb—do you think Darryl could ever become a scientist?

DAD: Well, Mother, I'm a little worried about Darryl. He's been acting kind of strange lately. *(Darryl starts sneaking across the back to get to the door. He's wearing boxer shorts on his head.)*

MOM: I think he may be having trouble making new friends.

DAD: *(without looking up from the newspaper)* Going out, son?

DARRYL: *(rather nervous)* Yeah, Dad, I'm going out with the guys for a couple of hours.

DAD: Okay, but don't be out late. Remember, it's a school night.

DARRYL: Yeah, I know.

MOM: *(turning around)* Darryl, dear, before you ... good grief! What do you have on your head?

DARRYL: *(trying to appear nonchalant)* Oh, it's just my new, uh, cap.

MOM: But they're ... they're ...

DAD: *(puts down the newspaper and sees Darryl)* Underwear!

DARRYL: Dad, they're from Jacques Pennae, and we prefer to call them "briefs." *(He rolls the "r." Dad just stares. Mother rushes to Darryl.)*

MOM: Oh, Darryl, do you have a fever? Did we spank you too much as a child?

DARRYL: Mom, I'm fine.

MOM: But the elastic is going to give you a rash.

DARRYL: Really, Mom, I'm fine! And they hide my acne.

DAD: Son, where do you wear your **hat?**

DARRYL: You're both acting like you've never seen anyone with briefs on his head before.

DAD: Well, we haven't! Have you?

DARRYL: Of course. *(appealingly)* Mom, everyone is wearing 'em now. It's the latest thing.

MOM: *(wringing her hands)* Oh, Darryl—what does your girl-friend think?

DARRYL: Mom, women love it. They think it makes a guy look great.

DAD: Young man, I don't want you to leave this house with those things on your head.

MOM: Darryl, will you wear long johns on your head in the winter?

DARRYL: Aw, c'mon, Mom. Look, Dad. Everyone is wearing them. I've got to have a pair or I won't fit in. Do you want your

only son to stand out like a sore thumb? I have to do what everyone else is doing or people won't like me.

MOM: Well, Herb, they do go quite nicely with his shirt.

DAD: *(with a big sigh)* Well, Darryl, I guess it's okay if you need them to belong, but make sure this group of people is worth belonging to. *(doorbell rings)*

DARRYL: Thanks, Dad. I gotta go. *(kisses Mom)* See ya later.

DAD: Just make sure you stick with **men's** briefs.
(Darryl meets his friends who both have boxer shorts on their heads and socks hanging off their ears.)
(freeze)

THE CABLE POLICE

THEME: Judgment

SCRIPTURE: As the weeds are pulled up and burned in the fire, so it will be at the end of the age. The Son of Man will send out his angels, and they will weed out of his kingdom everything that causes sin and all who do evil (Matthew 13:40-41).

SYNOPSIS: A man who illegally hooked himself up to cable TV is arrested by the cable police.

CHARACTERS:
Narrator
Francis (the homeowner)—tall, muscular type
Joe (the policeman)—short, swaggering kind of guy

PROPS: a chair, a TV or a box to represent one, a small pad of paper (similar to what police use for writing traffic tickets), handcuffs

(The scene opens with Francis watching football on TV. He is quite animated and involved in the game.)

NARRATOR: In Jesus' parable of the weeds, the wheat and the weeds grow up side by side, both enjoying the same sun and rain. But at the end of the story, the harvesters come and pull up the weeds, separate them from the wheat and burn them. Jesus tells us that the harvest represents the judgment that comes at the end of the age. It will take many people by surprise, much like what happened to a man named Francis who illegally hooked his TV up to cable.

FRANCIS: *(watching the TV)* Hit him again, he can still crawl!

(jumping out of his chair) Look out, he's still going for the goal line! *(collapses back into his chair)* I love having cable TV—this ESPN is great. Who would have thought they played such great football in Latvia? *(leans forward)* There he goes again! Tackle him, tackle him! *(knock on the door)*

FRANCIS: *(never taking his eyes off the TV)* Yeah, yeah, I'm coming. *(opens door and looks over Joe's head)* What? *(looks down)* Oh, what do you want?

JOE: *(looks at his pad)* Francis Tinyson?

FRANCIS: *(impatiently)* Yes.

JOE: 1423 King of Prussia Lane?

FRANCIS: *(more impatiently)* Yes, yes …

JOE: Are you watching Latvian Tag Team Football on ESPN?

FRANCIS: *(suddenly wary)* Why do you ask?

JOE: Answer the question please, Mr. Tinyson. Just before you came to the door, were you watching Latvian Tag Team Football on ESPN?

FRANCIS: Yes, I was. *(looking over Joe's head and squinting)* Why are all my neighbors getting into that blue police van? Hey, Bob! *(smiles and waves)*

JOE: Then you're under arrest under ordinance X9972B433I for hooking up your TV to cable and not paying for it. That's "X" as in xylophone, "B" as in Bob and "I" as in illegal.

FRANCIS: *(looking down at Joe)* You can arrest me for that?

JOE: I sure can. I'm a cable cop.

FRANCIS: But all I did was run a line from my neighbor Bob's house to my TV.

JOE: We got him, too. He was running a line from **his** neighbor's house. It turns out that only one house on the entire block has been paying for the use of cable.

FRANCIS: Only one house on this whole block?

JOE: Yep, all these houses look the same on the outside, but there's illegal activity going on inside some of them—like yours. Turn around and put your hands behind your back. *(slips handcuffs on Francis)*

FRANCIS: *(turning around)* But, but, you never warned me—it's not fair.

JOE: This is real, bucko. We did warn you. We had full-page ads in the paper and on the TV. We even had an amnesty week when you could join up and start paying and we wouldn't even ask how you got hooked up.

FRANCIS: Where are you taking me?

JOE: Down to the station to book you. *(starts to pull Francis out the door)*

FRANCIS: Marge, honey, I'm going out for a little while. I'll call.

(to Joe) I just did it so I could get WGN and watch the Cubs.

JOE: Sure, sure, that's what they all say. I guess you're out of luck—there's no TV at the jail.
(freeze)

NARRATOR: Francis knew that what he was doing was illegal, yet he chose to ignore the warnings. Whether or not we're ready for it, there is a day of judgment coming. The warning signs are everywhere, and no excuses will be accepted.

*P*art Three

COMPLETE SERVICES

In this section you'll find eight ready-to-use
creative services for a variety of church holidays
and for those times when you want to draw your
youth group or congregation together with
unique worship experiences.

A SERVICE OF SILENCE

*This service provides a unique experience
in silent corporate worship.*

PREPARATION

Gather Bibles, newsprint, markers, pens or pencils, paper, envelopes and candles. Practice singing "Be Still and Know" to the tune of "Amazing Grace."

THE SERVICE

● **Introduction**—Say: **In our modern, noisy world we seldom experience silence. Silent time was something Jesus valued. As you read the gospel accounts of Jesus' life, you'll find he often sought quiet in the mountains.**

This worship service uses quiet time. It may seem strange to experience so much silence. You may become aware of other sounds that might distract you from worship. Allow the silence to impact your life as you worship together.

● **A Song**—Have musicians from your youth group lead "Be Still and Know" to the tune of "Amazing Grace."

Be still and know that I am God.
Be still and know that I am God.
Be still and know that I am God.
Be still, be still, be still.

Sing the song again adding sign language. If no one in your group knows sign language, use these simple motions: Put a finger to your lips for "be still," point to your head for "and know" and point to the sky for "I am God."

Finally, "sing" the song again using only signs and no sound.

● **A Scripture**—Distribute Bibles. Point to a sheet of newsprint on which you have written "Read Psalm 46." After participants have silently read the psalm, write on the newsprint, "How important is this in my life?" Allow a full five minutes for reading and reflection.

● **A Note to God**—Give each participant a pen or pencil, a sheet of paper and an envelope. Write the following instruction on newsprint: "Write a letter to God communicating what you need from him. When you finish, place your letter in your envelope."

Allow three or four minutes for this activity.

● **An Offering to God**—Post a sheet of newsprint with the heading "Something I can offer to God." List examples such as loyalty, honesty and joy. Silently encourage participants to add their offerings to God on that same piece of newsprint. Allow two or three minutes for people to make their offerings.

● **Closing**—Silently indicate that worshipers are to join you in a circle. Give a candle to each person. Light your candle and then light the candle of the person next to you, indicating that he or she in turn will light the next person's candle. When all candles are lit, begin humming "Amazing Grace," which the service began with. Hum the song through twice.

To end the service, say "amen." Allow people to leave the worship area when they're inclined to do so. Once the quietness of the experience is broken, invite everyone to take a three-minute break after which you will regroup and reflect on the experience.

● **Reflection**—Depending on the size of your group, discuss these questions with the entire group or in clusters of three or four:

● **How did the silent worship experience feel to you?**

● **Were there moments the silence seemed strange? Which moments? Why?**

● **Where in your life do you experience silence?**

● **Is this the kind of experience you would like to have again? Why or why not?**

● **What was the most meaningful part of the worship? Explain.**

● **Do you need more silence in your life? Why or why not?**

Arlo Reichter

COMMISSIONING SERVICE

Use this service as a meaningful send-off for teams going to workcamps or mission projects.

PREPARATION

Read through the service and adapt the symbols and order of service to suit your situation. Retype your modified order of service and make copies for all the participants. As the service is written here, you'll need a Bible, printed music, a hammer, a paintbrush, a notebook, bread and a cup. Arrange to have various adults or elders present the symbols to the mission team. Have the mission team and the presenters stand in the front of the congregation.

When the mission team returns, consider presenting the service again. This time the mission team presents the symbols to the elders and tells the congregation how they used each of the symbols in the mission experience. This results in a powerful, moving worship service!

THE SERVICE

LEADER: The voice of the Lord calls to (destination of the mission team).

PEOPLE: Let us listen and pray to hear that voice.

MISSION TEAM: May we hear and respond to God's call in (destination).

PEOPLE: How can we, the members of God's family in this place, empower these workers?

ELDERS: We have pledged our financial and prayerful support. We now bring these symbols to illustrate our faith in God's ability to work miracles in and through this team.

ELDER #1: Accept this Bible and be a reminder of God's living Word to the people of (destination). Live and teach the scripture.

ELDER #2: Accept this music and use it to sing God's praise with the people you serve.

ELDER #3: Accept this hammer and use it to build community. Knock down the walls of gender, race, income and culture that separate us.

ELDER #4: Accept this paintbrush and use it to beautify and restore (destination). Cover the scars of our past indifference with the colors of God's love.

ELDER #5: Accept this notebook and use it to record what you see that you may learn from God's people in (destination).

PASTOR: Accept this bread and this cup and remember that we are all fed by Christ to feed Christ's world.

(Have the elders and pastor form a circle around the mission team.)

PASTOR: Let us pray: Lord God, we pray for these workers today. We ask that you would give them grace to be your ambassadors in our hurting world.

MISSION TEAM: Heavenly Father, accept our efforts when they please you and frustrate our attempts when they do not. Lead us in Christ to become worthy disciples, filled with the Spirit, as we respond to God's calling.

PEOPLE: Give us all grace, Lord, to hear your voice wherever and whenever you call to us. Empower us to step out here in (own locality) and proclaim your lordship over all of life. Send us, Lord, even as we send these workers. Through Christ our Lord we pray, amen.

Dave Carver

LOVE WILL FIND A WAY

*Members of God's family anonymously share their hurts and
pray for each other's healing.*

PREPARATION

Photocopy the responsive reading. Gather an offering plate, adhesive
bandages, pencils, red apples, plastic knives and a box. Rehearse the
skit "The Family." Collect tapes or CDs for background music.

THE SERVICE

● **Invocation**—Say: **Heavenly Father, be with us today as we explore new ways to walk in your love. Amen.**

● **Responsive Reading**—Read together the responsive reading, page
89.

● **Reverse Offering**—Rather than placing something *into* the offering
plate, everyone takes something *out* of it. The offering plate is filled with
adhesive bandages and pencils. Worshipers take one of each.

● **Remember Our Hurts**—Participants anonymously write on the
back of the bandage wrappers one problem or frustration they are currently facing. After they write their hurts on their bandage wrappers, have
worshipers bring them to the front of the room, place them in the offering plate and return to their seats.

Play background music during this portion of the service. Amy
Grant's "First Love" from *Never Alone* works well for this activity.

● **Apple Communion**—Give everyone a small red apple and a plastic knife. Say: **The red skin of your apple symbolizes the blood of**

Jesus. **The white part of the fruit symbolizes his body. Go around the room sharing small slices of your apple with other people as if you were sharing Christ.**

During this activity, play "Love Will Be Our Home" from *Make His Praise Glorious* by Sandi Patti. Have worshipers deposit their apple cores and knives in a box as the song draws to a close. Then have everyone stand in a circle and sing "I Love You, Lord" (#46 in *The Group Songbook*).

● **Share Our Hurts**—Have worshipers form pairs and come to the front of the room. Partners will each remove one adhesive bandage (not their own) from the offering plates at the front. Have pairs move to a quiet place in the room where they will pray for the hurts represented by the bandages they're holding.

You may want to use Steve Green's "Only Jesus—Calvary's Love" from *For God and God Alone* as background music for this activity.

● **Prayer Reminder**—Have worshipers return to their seats. Say: **Tear open the bandage you're holding and stick it on your shoulder as a reminder to keep on praying for the person and the hurt it represents.** As worshipers are putting on their bandages, read aloud Galatians 6:2.

● **Skit**—Perform the skit "The Family," page 90.

● **Responsive Reading**—Have the characters from the skit lead the congregation in a second reading of the responsive reading.

● **Closing**—Have everyone join hands. Pray: **Lord Jesus, help us walk in your love this week. Amen.**

Michael Capps

RESPONSIVE READING

Paraphrase of 1 John 4:18a, 20-21; and 1 Corinthians 13

LEADER: There is no fear in love, because perfect love drives out fear. If a person says, "I love God," yet hates his brother or sister, that person is a liar. You see, those who don't love a brother or sister they've seen can't love a God they haven't seen. Therefore, those who really want to love God must love their brothers and sisters.

YOUTH: Though I may be able to speak French, Spanish or Japanese and even rap with the angels, if I don't have love, my speech is no more than a busted guitar or a smashed CD.

LEADER: I may preach like Billy Graham, have the brains of Einstein or have all the faith needed to send a space shuttle into orbit, but if I don't have love, I am nothing.

YOUTH: I may give the shirt off my back and even smash my heavy metal albums to please my parents, but if I don't have love, it does me no good.

LEADER: Love is tolerant and tender; love is not stuck-up or up-tight; love is not snotty, snobbish or touchy; love isn't the least bit pessimistic.

YOUTH: Love doesn't swim in the gutter or hunt for gossip. It's happy with the truth.

LEADER: Love never gives up. Its faith, hope and patience never fail.

YOUTH: Love can outlast "the Energizer," Duracell and even life itself.

LEADER: People will talk forever but never get things done. Rock groups and sports heroes may shake the world but are soon forgotten.

YOUTH: When perfect truth comes, life begins to take on meaning. And when love comes, the meaning of life is complete.

LEADER: When I was a dumb kid, my whole life was wrapped up in immature selfishness and egotism, but now I have grown up and matured. I am embarrassed by vain self-centeredness.

YOUTH: Sometimes life seems like crazy mirrors at a carnival; things are twisted, distorted and fuzzy. But one day God will open our eyes, and then we'll be able to see life as he does.

LEADER: Meanwhile, our survival kit must be supplied with faith, hope and love.

ALL: Love is the greatest so put love first.

Permission to photocopy this responsive reading granted for local church use. Copyright © Group Publishing, Inc., Box 481, Loveland, CO 80539.

THE FAMILY

Cast: man, woman, teenage girl, teenage guy

(Position all four characters at the back of the room. The man and woman walk toward the front of the room fighting.)

MAN: Why isn't dinner ever on the table when I get home?

WOMAN: Because you get home five minutes after I do. If you want instant food, go to McDonald's!

MAN: I'd probably get better stuff than I get here.

WOMAN: And I'd probably have a better evening if you were out of here. Feel free to leave.

MAN: Tryin' to get rid of me? Forget it!

WOMAN: Fine. Then you can empty the dishwasher and set the table.

MAN: Do you boss everybody this way, or is it special treatment you save for me?

WOMAN: I've had it with you!

(Man and woman turn back to back, arms crossed and freeze. Immediately the teenage girl walks toward the front, yelling at the man and woman.)

GIRL: Why can't I go to the party? You don't like any of my friends! I really need some new jeans! Everyone else is going to the mall. Why can't I? That's not fair!

(The girl gets right up in the woman's face, a few inches from her nose, and then freezes. Immediately the teenage guy jumps up and stalks toward the front, yelling at the man and woman.)

GUY: Hey, thanks for killing my social life! You never let me get my hands on the car! I cut the grass and do the dishes for a measly little allowance. Maybe I should just leave so you'd be stuck with all the lousy jobs you always pawn off on me!

(The guy moves within a few inches of the man's nose and then freezes.)

MAN and WOMAN: (to the guy and girl) As long as you live in this house, you'll do what I say!

(All freeze. Play Amy Grant's "If These Walls Could Speak" from Lead Me On. *At the close of the song, all four characters give each other hugs of forgiveness.)*

Permission to photocopy this skit granted for local church use. Copyright © Group Publishing, Inc., Box 481, Loveland, CO 80539.

THE SYMBOLS OF CHRISTMAS

This Christmas service presents the significance of Jesus' birth through symbols, songs and scriptures.

PREPARATION

Enlist teenagers and upper-elementary children to make these six symbols: a star, a crown, an angel, a sheep, a gift and a cross. They may be presented as banners or as large, colorful, three-dimensional objects, large enough to be seen easily from all parts of the congregation. Choose children or teenagers to display each of the symbols at the appropriate time in the service.

Arrange for readers. One teenager might be dressed as a prophet for the Isaiah passages. The leader's parts may be read by one person, or you might use a different leader for each of the six sections of the service. You might want a "live" angel as the angel symbol *and* as a reader. Consider planting other readers in the congregation.

The songs can be performed by a youth choir or led by teenage musicians. You may wish to have some of the songs presented as instrumental or vocal solos.

THE SERVICE

LEADER: We welcome you to our time of worship. Our theme for this service is the symbols of Christmas. God uses many different symbols to show us what he's like. We'll learn what six different symbols tell us about Jesus. Let's sing our opening song as a prayer.

● **SONG:** "Open Our Eyes" (#50 in *The Group Songbook, The Group*

Songbook: *Split-Channel Cassette, Vol. 2)*
(Display the star.)

LEADER: A star is a symbol of light. Long before the birth of Jesus, the prophet Isaiah foretold the coming of a great light into our world that was dark with sin.

READER: The people walking in the dark will see a great light. On those who live in the land of gloom a light will shine. Arise, shine, for your light has come, and the Lord's glory is shining on you. Darkness still covers the earth and thick darkness the people, but the Lord will rise over you, and his glory will appear over you. People will come to your light, and as you shine, kings will come near *(from Isaiah 9:2; 60:1-3)*.

LEADER: When Jesus was born, a beautiful bright star appeared in the sky and led the wise men to the baby. The Bible tells us that the star went before them and came to rest over the place where Jesus was. While Jesus was on earth, he told people that he was the light of the world.

READER: Jesus said, "I am the light of the world; he who follows me will not walk in darkness, but will have the light of life" *(from John 8:12)*.

LEADER: Jesus also said that we, his disciples, are the light of the world. We are to let our light shine for others so they will praise God. Let's join in prayer: Jesus, thank you for being the light of this dark world. I want your light to shine through me so others will know I belong to you! Amen.

● **SONG:** "Shine on My Life With Your Love" (#5 in *The Group Songbook, The Group Songbook: Split-Channel Cassette, Vol. 1)*
(Display the crown.)

LEADER: The prophet Isaiah spoke of a king to come who would be far greater than King David. Listen to his words.

READER: A child will be born for us, a son will be given to us, and the government will be on his shoulder, and he will be called Wonderful Counselor, Mighty God, Everlasting Father, Prince of Peace. His government will grow, and there will be endless peace, to establish his rule on David's throne and to uphold it with justice and righteousness now and forever. The zeal of the Lord of armies will do this *(from Isaiah 9:6-7)*.

LEADER: When the wise men came to Jerusalem following the star, do you remember who they said they were looking for? When Jesus was nailed to the cross, do you remember what the sign above him said?

● **SONG:** "King of Kings" (#43 in *The Group Songbook, The Group Songbook: Split-Channel Cassette, Vol. 1)*

LEADER: The Bible tells us that when Jesus comes to earth again at the end of the world, he will come as king with great power and majesty. He will reign forever and ever.

READER: "I am the Alpha and the Omega," says the Lord God, "who is and who was and who is to come, the Almighty" *(from Revelation 1:8)*.

LEADER: Let's join in prayer: Jesus, I know that you are the greatest king who ever lived. I know you are a good king who loves me more than anyone in the whole world does. I want you to be my king and rule in my heart.

● **SONG:** "We Will Glorify" (#1 in *The Group Songbook, The Group Songbook: Split-Channel Cassette, Vol. 2)*

(Display the angel.)

LEADER: Angels are another important Christmas symbol. God used his angels many times to bring his messages to people on earth. The angels brought good news to the people! The angel Gabriel came to Mary and told her she would have a son.

READER: "Don't be afraid, Mary," the angel told her. "God is good to you. You see, you will conceive and have a son, and you will call him Jesus. He will be great and will be called the Son of the Most High God. And the Lord will give him the throne of his ancestor David. He will be king over the people of Jacob forever, and his kingdom will never end" *(from Luke 1:30-33)*.

LEADER: The angel of the Lord appeared to the shepherds the night Jesus was born and told them the good news.

READER: And the angel said to them, "Be not afraid for behold, I bring you good news of a great joy which will come to all the people; for to you is born this day in the city of David, a Savior, who is Christ the Lord" *(from Luke 2:10-11)*.

● **SONG:** "Angels We Have Heard on High" *(Group's Christmas Caroling Kit)*

LEADER: After Jesus rose from the dead, angels appeared and told his disciples that he was alive again. And when Jesus ascended into heaven, angels also appeared and told his disciples that he would return to earth someday. The angels brought good news about Jesus to the people. God also calls **us** to bring the good news about Jesus to people everywhere. That includes our family, neighbors and people at school or work. We are special messengers of God's love to the world. Take a moment now to share the peace and love of Jesus with the people around you. Shake hands with at least six people and say, "The peace and love of Jesus be with you!"

(Signal the end of the handshaking with the introduction to the next song.)

● **SONG:** "Go, Tell It on the Mountain" *(Group's Christmas Caroling Kit)*

(Display the sheep.)

LEADER: Our next symbol is a sheep. Did you know that in the Bible God compares us to sheep? Because of our sin, we are lost and cut off from God. We are helpless and dumb—we don't know how to take care of ourselves and we can't get rid of our sin. The prophet Isaiah talks about us being like sheep.

READER: We have all gone astray like sheep. Every one of us has turned to go his own way, and the Lord has punished him for the sins of all of us *(from Isaiah 53:6)*.

LEADER: God punished Jesus for your sins and mine. While we are called sheep in the Bible, Jesus is called the good shepherd.

READER: Jesus said, "I am the good shepherd. The good shepherd lays down his life for the sheep" *(from John 10:11)*.

LEADER: We need Jesus to save us from our sins and to care for us. We need him as our good shepherd every day. Let's sing about our good shepherd.

● **SONG:** "The Lord Is My Shepherd" (round)

(Display the gift.)

LEADER: We give and receive gifts at Christmas. They're meant to remind us of the gift God gave us that first Christmas.

READER: For God so loved the world that he gave his only son, that whoever believes in him should not perish but have eternal life *(from John 3:16)*.

LEADER: God kept his promise to send a Savior. He sent the very best by sending his only son, Jesus. Jesus is God's Christmas gift to you and me and all people! Let's pray together and thank God for his wonderful gift to us: Dear God, thank you so much for loving me. Thank you for sending your son, Jesus, to be my Savior. Jesus, I love you. Amen.

● **SONG:** "Away in a Manger" *(Group's Christmas Caroling Kit)*

(Display the cross.)

LEADER: The cross is the symbol of God's love. We do not deserve his love. But God loves us so much that he sent Jesus to die for us. The Bible explains it this way:

READER: But God shows his love for us in that while we were yet sinners Christ died for us *(from Romans 5:8)*.

LEADER: Jesus' death on the cross was part of God's plan to send a Savior. Christmas, Good Friday and Easter are all part of the same package—God's gift of love for us.

● **SONG:** "Jesus Loves Me" (#69 in *The Group Songbook, The Group Songbook: Split-Channel Cassette, Vol. 3*)

LEADER: Let's go back over these symbols and review what they tell us about Jesus.

(Have the symbol-bearers hold up their symbols as each one is reviewed.)

LEADER: ● The **star** shows where Jesus was and reminds us that Jesus is the light of the world.

    ● The **crown** reminds us that Jesus is our king; he will reign for ever!

    ● The **angel** brought good news about Jesus to the people.

    ● The **sheep** reminds us that we are like sheep and need a savior.

    ● The **gift** reminds us that God gave his very best gift when he gave us Jesus.

    ● The **cross** reminds us of God's love and of Jesus' death for you and me.

Just as each of these symbols centers around Jesus, our preparations for the Christmas season must have Jesus in the center. He is the reason we celebrate Christmas.

READER: The angel said to Joseph, "She will have a son and you will call him Jesus, because he will save his people from their sins." All this happened so that what the Lord said through the prophet would come true: "The virgin will conceive and have a son, and he will be called Immanuel, which means 'God-with-us' " *(from Matthew 1:21-22).*

READER: And being found in human form, he humbled himself and became obedient unto death, even death on a cross. Therefore, God has highly exalted him and bestowed on him the name which is above every name, that at the name of **Jesus** every knee should bow, in heaven and on earth and under the earth, and every tongue confess that **Jesus Christ is Lord,** to the glory of God the Father *(from Philippians 2:8-11).*

● **SONG:** "O Come, All Ye Faithful" *(Group's Christmas Caroling Kit)*

Linda Joyce Heaner

Permission to photocopy this service granted for local church use.
Copyright © Group Publishing, Inc., Box 481, Loveland, CO 80539.

FESTIVAL OF LIGHT

This post-Christmas, or Epiphany, burning of the greens encourages worshipers to take Jesus' light to the world.

PREPARATION

Assign the readings and scriptures to different young people. Plan to hold the service in a place where you can safely burn the evergreens used to decorate the church during the Christmas season. Gather the evergreens to be burned. You might want to invite church members to bring their Christmas trees and greens as well.

THE SERVICE

● **Introduction**—Epiphany means "shine forth." The glory of our God shines forth in the Christ in the manger, the Christ in the temple, the Christ with his friends, the Christ on the cross and the Christ in each of us. Many churches bring the post-Christmas season to a close with the Transfiguration story as a reminder that we all have bright "God-moments" but are called to take the light into the world—our world. That's the tough part. Our strength is in Jesus' promise, "I will be with you always." In light of that promise, let us shine!

LEADER: We gather around the evergreens, now dried-up symbols of our celebrations with families and friends.

READER: Reminders also of how God graciously sent Jesus to another tree so our lives could be full of light and warmth.

LEADER: As the evergreens burn brightly and the limbs crackle in the flames, so should our lives burn with love for our God and reflect our

Creator, Redeemer and Sanctifier.

(Light the fire.)

READER: Then God commanded, "Let there be light"—and light appeared. God was pleased with what he saw. Then he separated the light from the darkness *(from Genesis 1:3-5).*

LEADER: I'd like several people to share in one sentence your favorite Christmas tradition from your family or church.

(Pause a moment as worshipers share.)

READER: There the angel of the Lord appeared to him as a flame coming from the middle of a bush. Moses saw that the bush was on fire, but that it was not burning up *(from Exodus 3:2).*

LEADER: Now I'd like you to share a time when you felt very close to God during this season.

(Pause a moment as worshipers share.)

READER: Arise, shine, for your light has come, and the glory of the Lord rises on you *(from Isaiah 60:1).*

RESPONSIVE READING—FROM INTERROBANG

VOICE #1: Men, women, students on the run,

VOICE #2: Stop a minute, people, and watch a satellite, a star, a sun, a signal of greater light to come.

VOICE #3: We can see the dark and evil forces of our society invading human lives like the plagues of long ago.

ALL: And so we call you, God, to unveil yourself once more

VOICE #1: And let the fire of your light, the sun in your son,

VOICE #2: Burn through us and shrivel that evil into smaller and smaller fragments

VOICE #3: Until nothing is left but the memory.

ALL: Come in, God, and make this a hot, bright day and a warm tomorrow!

(Reprinted from Interrobang by Norman Habel, copyright © 1969 Fortress Press.
Used by permission of Augsburg Fortress.)

READER: The people living in darkness have seen a great light; on those living in the land of the shadow of death a light has dawned *(Matthew 4:16)*.

LEADER: The light of Jesus, the Christ, brightens the darkness of our shame, fear, guilt and failure with forgiveness and hope.

READER: Let our light shine before others, that they may see our good deeds and praise our Father in heaven *(from Matthew 5:16)*.

LEADER: We are to reflect God's grace and glory.

READER: It's time for us to shine!

RESPONSIVE READING: WALK IN THE LIGHT

VOICE #1: Wait a minute! Not so fast! It's not easy to reflect God's light. I mean, what about at school? Not many kids talk about God.

VOICE #2: I even have trouble when I leave church on Sunday. It's like I turn out the lights when I leave.

VOICE #3: There are times I like the darkness better than the light. I can hide many things about me in the darkness.

VOICE #1: I know what you mean. I don't want everyone to know all that I do. I guess there's a little darkness in each of us.

ALL: Yeah!

READER: When Jesus spoke again to the people, he said, "I am the light of the world. Whoever follows me will never walk in darkness, but will have the light of life" *(John 8:12)*.

ALL: Uh-oh!

VOICE #2: But just a little darkness wouldn't be so bad.

READER: I have come into the world as a light, so that no one who believes in me should stay in darkness *(John 12:46)*.

VOICE #3: Then what will we do?

ALL: Let our light shine!

(All join in singing this "Light Song" to the tune of "Amazing Grace.")

"Light Song"
Light-house
Soft-glow
Ne-on
Christ-mas
Desk-lamp
Light-ning
Can-dle
Flash-ing
Am-ber
Bon-fire
Spot-light
Traf-fic
Run-way
Je-sus

Dick Hardel

Permission to photocopy this service granted for local church use.
Copyright © Group Publishing, Inc., Box 481, Loveland, CO 80539.

*B*EFORE CHRIST'S CRUCIFIXION

This service allows worshipers to experience the sights, sounds and feelings of the Last Supper and the Crucifixion.

*P*REPARATION

Have kids help you make a cross from rough wood. It's particularly meaningful to construct the cross from two pieces of a Christmas tree trunk. Plan to begin the service in a lower-level room of the church where the lighting is fairly dim. Place the following items on a table in the center of the worship area: the cross, enough sixteenpenny nails for each participant to have one, a hammer, a towel, a pottery basin filled with warm water, a candle and matches. Arrange chairs for the worshipers in a circle around the table. For large groups, arrange chairs in concentric circles and have one towel and basin for every 30 worshipers.

Place a candle, a Bible and the communion elements in the darkened "upper room" or sanctuary. Assign teenagers to read Isaiah 53:1-9, John 13:1-7 and a poem about the cross or the mystery of communion. Choose from the poems listed below or ask a creative writer in your group to create a poem of his or her own. Kids can also lead or accompany the songs. It is best to speak as little as possible during this service and to simply let the Holy Spirit speak through the actions.

*T*HE SERVICE

● **Introduction**—Play meditative music as worshipers enter. Begin the service by holding up the cross. If the cross is made from the trunk of a

Christmas tree, point out that the tree we use to celebrate the birth of Jesus becomes a symbol of the cruelty of sin.

● **Song**—"The Old Rugged Cross"

● **Reading**—A poem about the cross or the mystery of Communion such as "Craftsman" by Luci Shaw or "At Communion" by Madeleine L'Engle (both from *The Treasury of Christian Poetry,* Fleming H. Revell Company).

● **Nailprints**—Distribute nails and have worshipers press the cold, raw iron into the palms of their hands. (Placing the nails in a refrigerator before the service makes the effect even more powerful.) While worshipers hold the nails, have the assigned person read Isaiah 53:1-9. Then, slowly and dramatically, pound a nail into the cross.

● **Song**—"Were You There?"

● **Hand Washing**—Since foot washing is not part of our culture, most groups might be more comfortable with a hand washing service. The effect of being cleansed and ministered to can be very powerful. Have the assigned person read John 13:1-7. Ask an assistant to carry the pottery basin of warm water and the towel. The leader dips each person's hands into warm water and then dries them with the towel. Large groups will need more than one leader and assistant.

● **Communion**—Say to the group: **Let us prepare for the feast. Follow me to the upper room.**

Light a candle and lead the worshipers up to the darkened sanctuary. The candlelight procession creates a sense of anticipation and intimacy. Lead the worshipers to a table in the front of the sanctuary where you have placed a candle, a Bible and the communion elements. Light the candle and ask everyone to stand around the table.

Pass the candle you're holding to the person who will read Mark 14:17-25. Then, in silence, take the bread, break off a piece for yourself and pass the loaf around the circle. After eating the bread, pass the cup in the manner most appropriate for your group.

Read Psalm 136 as a litany. Explain that at each pause worshipers will repeat the phrase "His love endures forever." Then join hands in the circle and sing "Alleluia."

● **Benediction**—Say: **Peace to all of you who are in Christ** *(1 Peter 5:14b).* **Go in silence.**

Bob Keffer

EASTER SERVICE: GOD KEEPS HIS PROMISES!

This service draws worshipers into a dramatic, multisensory retelling of Jesus' resurrection.

PREPARATION

Gather Bible costumes for two women, small wooden boxes to serve as spice boxes and white robes for angel costumes. Recruit four youth group members to prepare the drama in the introduction. Have a youth choir prepare "The Easter Song" by The 2nd Chapter of Acts. Arrange for soloists to sing "Were You There?" and "Great Is Thy Faithfulness." Prepare heart-shaped handouts with a cross in the center and the words "I love you" written on the crossbar. Ask three or four people to be prepared to tell the congregation how God has proven faithful to his promises in their lives.

Remove all decoration from the front of the sanctuary; make it as barren as possible. Place a microphone for the narrator and singers out of sight at the rear of the sanctuary or in a balcony. Place several Easter lilies out of sight of the worshipers but easily accessible.

THE SERVICE

● **Introduction**—The sanctuary is dark as worshipers gather. From a balcony or the rear of the sanctuary, a soloist sings the first two verses of "Were You There?" Then four youth group members present the following drama:

(Two robed women enter carrying spice boxes. They walk mournfully and hesitantly toward the front of the church. As they walk, the narrator speaks from the rear of the church.)

NARRATOR: On the first day of the week, very early in the morning, the women took the spices they had prepared and went to the tomb.

WOMAN #1: We've got the spices and perfumes we need for Jesus' body, but who will roll the stone away?

WOMAN #2: Look! The stone **is** rolled away! Have they taken his body?

(Two men in white angel costumes appear. Put a spotlight on them if possible. The women are visibly frightened.)

ANGELS: Don't be afraid. I know you're looking for Jesus who was crucified. Why do you look for the living among the dead? He's not here, he has risen, just as he said! Come and see the place where he lay. Then go quickly and tell his disciples, "He has risen from the dead and is going ahead of you into Galilee. You'll see Him there!"

(The women rush out, filled with excitement, addressing the congregation as they go.)

WOMEN: He's risen! Jesus is alive! He's risen!

● **The Celebration**—The youth choir enters singing "The Easter Song." During the singing, children or family groups carry in Easter lilies and place them on and around the altar. As they decorate the altar, the lights gradually come up until the church is fully lit and all the flowers are in place. The visual impact of the altar area going from dark and empty to bright and beautiful is very moving.

● **Song**—"Christ the Lord Is Risen Today"

● **Reading**—The Beginning of the Promise

LEADER: Our God keeps his promises! Back in the Garden of Eden, he promised Adam and Eve that he would send a Savior. He promised Abraham that through his descendants all the nations of the earth would be blessed. In the fullness of time, God sent his Son to live on this earth. An angel appeared to Joseph and told him, "Do not be afraid to take Mary home as your wife, because what is conceived in her is from the Holy Spirit. She will give birth to a son, and you are to give him the name Jesus, because he will save his people from their sins. They will call his name Immanuel, which means 'God with us.' "

● **Song**—"Jesus, Name Above All Names"

● **Readings**—Jesus' Promises

LEADER: While Jesus was alive, he made promises to his disciples.

(Readers may stand and read from various places in the congregation.)

READER #1: The Son of Man is going to be betrayed into the hands of men. They will kill him, and after three days he will rise *(Mark 9:31).*

READER #2: In my Father's house are many rooms ... I am going there to prepare a place for you. And ... I will come back and take you to be with me that you also may be where I am *(John 14:2-3).*

READER #3: Because I live, you also will live *(John 14:19b).*

● **Song**—"I Know That My Redeemer Lives"

● **Sharing God's Promises**

LEADER: God still keeps his promises today. Some members of our congregation are living proof of that.

(Have three or four people briefly share a promise from the Bible that's important to them and tell how God has worked in their lives.)

LEADER: Now we'd like to give everyone an opportunity to share a promise from God's Word that's special to you. Form a trio with people near you. In your trios, share God's promises and tell why they're important to you.

(Have instrumental background music playing as people share. Close the sharing time with the introduction to the solo.)

● **Solo**—"Great Is Thy Faithfulness." *(Have the congregation join the soloist in singing the song or chorus a second time.)*

● **The Greatest Promise**

LEADER: Perhaps God's greatest promise is a familiar one. Let's say John 3:16 together: For God so loved the world that he gave his one and only Son, that whoever believes in him shall not perish but have eternal life.

LEADER: Why did God send Jesus to die on the cross?

Because he loves me. Because he loves you.

Let's proclaim this truth together. I'll ask the question and you answer: Because he loves me!

Why did God send Jesus to die on the cross?

PEOPLE: Because he loves me!

LEADER: Why did God send Jesus to die on the cross?

PEOPLE: Because he loves me!

LEADER: This time, proclaim this answer to those around you: Because he loves **you!**

Why did God send Jesus to die on the cross?

PEOPLE: Because he loves **you!**

● **Songs**—"Jesus Loves Me" and "Oh, How He Loves You and Me" *(As the congregation sings, have youth group members hand out hearts with a cross drawn on them and the words "I love you" written on the crossbar.)*

● **Closing Prayer**—Thanks to God for his faithfulness in keeping his promises, for sending Jesus, for raising him from the dead and for the inheritance we will receive in heaven. Amen!

● **Closing Song**—"Lord We Praise You" or "He Is Lord"

Linda Joyce Heaner

A CELEBRATION OF JESUS' LIFE

This service celebrates the whole of Jesus' life from birth through resurrection.

PREPARATION

Use youth group members to help with the music and to do the readings. You may wish to use the same three readers during the whole service or to use a different trio of readers for each section. Having the readers in Bible costumes creates a nice effect. Some of the readings work well as dramas.

THE SERVICE

LEADER: I am the resurrection and the life. He who believes in me shall never die *(from John 11:25)*.

PEOPLE: He is the first and the last, and the living one, he died, but behold, he is alive forevermore *(from Revelation 1:17-18)*.

READER #1: In the beginning was the Word, and the Word was with God, and the Word was God. He was with God in the beginning.

READER #2: Through him all things were made; without him nothing was made that has been made. In him was life, and that life was the light of men.

READER #3: The light shines in the darkness, but the darkness has not understood it *(John 1:1-5)*.

PEOPLE: Thank you, Jesus, for bringing your light into the world.

LEADER: Shake hands with at least three people and say, "I greet you in light of Jesus' love."

(Pause a moment as worshipers greet each other.)

JESUS' BIRTH

READER #1: The Lord himself will give you a sign: The virgin will be with child and will give birth to a son, and will call him Immanuel *(Isaiah 7:14)*.

● **SONG:** "O Come, All Ye Faithful" *(Group's Christmas Caroling Kit)*

READER #3: So Joseph also went up from the town of Nazareth in Galilee to Judea, to Bethlehem the town of David, because he belonged to the house and line of David. He went there to register with Mary, who was pledged to be married to him and was expecting a child. While they were there, the time came for the baby to be born, and she gave birth to her firstborn, a son. She wrapped him in cloths and placed him in a manger, because there was no room for them in the inn *(Luke 2:4-7)*.

● **SONG:** "Joy to the World" *(Group's Christmas Caroling Kit)*

READER #2: And there were shepherds living out in the fields nearby, keeping watch over their flocks at night. An angel of the Lord appeared to them, and the glory of the Lord shone around them, and they were terrified. But the angel said to them,

READER #3: Do not be afraid. I bring you good news of great joy that will be for all the people. Today in the town of David a Savior has been born to you; he is Christ the Lord *(Luke 2:8-11)*.

READER:#1: The shepherds returned, glorifying and praising God for all the things they had heard and seen, which were just as they had been told *(Luke 2:20)*.

● **SONG:** "Go, Tell It on the Mountain" *(Group's Christmas Caroling Kit)*

ALL: Help us respond to your call with the same sense of purpose and excitement shown by the shepherds long ago. Give us courage and faith to follow you.

JESUS' LIFE

READER #2: Jesus went through all the towns and villages, teaching in their synagogues, preaching the good news of the kingdom and healing every disease and sickness *(Matthew 9:35)*.

READER #3: The people were amazed at his teaching, because he taught them as one who had authority, not as the teachers of the law *(Mark 1:22)*.

LEADER: Tell someone sitting near you one thing that amazes you about Jesus' teaching.

(Pause for a moment as worshipers share.)

LEADER: James and John, the sons of Zebedee came to Jesus.

READERS #2 and #3: Teacher, we want you to do for us whatever we ask.

READER #1: What do you want me to do for you?

READERS #2 and #3: Let one of us sit at your right and the other at your left in your glory.

READER #1: You don't know what you are asking. Can you drink the cup I drink or be baptized with the baptism I am baptized with?

READERS #2 and #3: We can.

READER #1: You will drink the cup I drink and be baptized with the baptism I am baptized with, but to sit at my right or left is not for me to grant. These places belong to those for whom they have been prepared *(from Mark 10:35-40)*.

● **SONG:** "I Have Decided to Follow Jesus" (#60 in *The Group Songbook)*

LEADER: Tell someone sitting close to you about a time when it was difficult for you to follow Jesus but you did it anyway.

(Pause for a moment as worshipers share.)

THE FINAL WEEK

LEADER: When they brought the colt to Jesus and threw their cloaks over it, he sat on it. Many people spread their cloaks on the road, while others spread branches they had cut in the fields. Those who went ahead and those who followed shouted,

PEOPLE: Hosanna! Blessed is he who comes in the name of the Lord! *(Mark 11:7-9).*

● **SONG:** "Hosanna, Loud Hosanna"

LEADER: And he took bread, gave thanks and broke it, and gave it to them saying,

READER #1: This is my body given for you; do this in remembrance of me.

LEADER: In the same way, after supper he took the cup, saying,

READER #1: This cup is the new covenant in my blood, which is poured out for you *(Luke 22:19-20).*

● **SONG:** "Let Us Break Bread Together"

READER #2: They brought Jesus to the place called Golgotha (which means The Place of the Skull).

READER #3: Then they offered him wine mixed with myrrh, but he did not take it.

READER #2: And they crucified him *(Mark 15:22-24a).*

LEADER: Close your eyes and picture in your mind the blackest, most discouraging moment of your life. *(Pause.)* Now take that black moment and place it at the foot of the cross where Jesus is hanging. *(Pause.)* With that picture fixed in your mind, join me in singing the first verse of "Were You There?"

● **SONG:** "Were You There?" (first verse)

LEADER: Early on the first day of the week, while it was still dark, Mary Magdalene went to the tomb and saw that the stone had been removed from the entrance.

READER #3: So she came running to Simon Peter and the other disciple, the one Jesus loved, and said,

READER #2: They have taken the Lord out of the tomb, and we don't know where they have put him! *(John 20:1-2).*

● **SONG:** "Low in the Grave He Lay" or remaining verses of "Were You There?"

READER #3: Mary stood outside the tomb crying. As she wept, she bent over to look into the tomb and saw two angels in white, seated where Jesus' body had been, one at the head and the other at the foot. They asked her,

LEADER: Woman, why are you crying?

READER #2: They have taken my Lord away and I don't know where they have put him.

READER #3: At this, she turned around and saw Jesus standing there, but she did not realize that it was Jesus.

READER #1: Woman, why are you crying? Who is it you are looking for?

READER #3: Thinking he was the gardener, she said,

READER #2: Sir, if you have carried him away, tell me where you have put him, and I will get him.

READER #3: Jesus said to her,

READER #1: Mary.

READER #3: She turned to him and cried out,

READER #2: Rabboni! [rah-BONE-eye] *(from John 20:11-16).*

● **SONG:** "Christ the Lord Is Risen Today"

BENEDICTION

LEADER: Lift up your hearts.

PEOPLE: We lift them up to the Lord.

LEADER: He is risen!

PEOPLE: He is risen indeed!

LEADER: May the risen Christ go with you!

PEOPLE: And with you also. Alleluia!

ALL: Amen.

J. Brent Bill

Permission to photocopy this service granted for local church use.
Copyright © Group Publishing, Inc., Box 481, Loveland, CO 80539.